Driving Theory Practice for 2016

Contents:

Page 2: Theory Test Questions
Page 111: Answers
Page 119: Answer Explanations

Practice for the car driving theory test with the questions from the DVSA revision question bank. This book contains over 500 multiple choice questions for you to practice, as well as the answers and explanations for every question.

1. At which crossing are cyclists allowed to cross with pedestrians?
a) Toucan crossing
b) Zebra crossing
c) Pelican crossing
d) None

2. What type of emergency vehicle uses a light that flashes green?
a) Bomb disposal
b) Ambulance
c) Doctor's car
d) Waste disposal

3. Why is it bad to drive in neutral for a long time?
a) You will have less control
b) You will be moving too slowly
c) Your engine may start revving
d) It damages the suspension

4. You're driving down a narrow country road. What is the best way to pass a cyclist?
a) As quickly as possible
b) Very slowly
c) By allowing enough space as you pass
d) Honk to let them know you're there

5. A bus lane does not show any times of operation. What does this mean?
a) The bus lane is never in operation
b) The bus lane is in operation for all hours of the day
c) The hours of operation for the bus lane are 9am - 5pm
d) Only cyclists may use the bus lane

6. Who are diamond shaped road signs directed to?
a) Taxis
b) Buses
c) Lorries
d) Trams

7. How deep can your tyre tread depth legally be?
a) 3.2mm
b) 1.6mm
c) 1.1mm
d) 2.7mm

8. How much more fuel is used when driving at 70mph as opposed to 50mph?
a) 50%
b) 10%
c) 5%
d) 30%

9. What level should you fill your car battery to?
a) Half way up
b) The top
c) Just below the cell plates
d) Just above the cell plates

10. What is the minimum stopping distance at 70mph on a dry road?
a) 50 metres
b) 73 metres
c) 90 metres
d) 140 metres

11. What should you do first if you break down in a tunnel?
a) Call the police
b) Switch on your hazard warning lights and turn off the engine
c) Wave down other traffic
d) Call a friend to come and help

12. What should you do when a smart motorway is operating?
a) You should stop and wait for further instructions
b) You must obey the speed limits shown
c) Leave the motorway at the next exit
d) Stay in the right hand lane

13. What document may a police officer ask you for after a collision?
a) Vehicle registration document
b) Driving license
c) MOT certificate
d) Driving test certificate

14. At what distance must you be able to read a number plate?
a) 5 metres
b) 10 metres
c) 15.5 metres
d) 20.5 metres

15. The reflective studs between a motorway and the slip road are what colour?
a) Blue
b) White
c) Green
d) Amber

16. Usually, what lane should you use on a three lane motorway?
a) Middle
b) Right
c) The hard shoulder
d) Left

17. Where on a motorway may you find a crawler lane?
a) Just before an exit
b) When you are coming on to the motorway
c) On a steep gradient
d) Near a service station

18. Who must not use a motorway?

a) Learner drivers

b) Elderly people

c) Newly insured full-license drivers

d) Anyone under the age of 21

19. What should you do before making a U-turn?

a) Give an arm signal as well as using your indicators

b) Check signs to see that U-turns are permitted

c) Look over your shoulder for a final check

d) Select a higher gear than normal

20. In which of these situations should you avoid overtaking?

a) Just after a bend

b) In a one-way street

c) On a 30 mph road

d) Approaching a dip in the road

21. Your mobile phone rings while you're travelling. What should you do?

a) Stop immediately

b) Answer it immediately

c) Ignore it

d) Pull up at the nearest kerb

22. What should you do when you're approaching traffic lights that have been on green for some time?

a) Accelerate hard

b) Maintain your speed

c) Be ready to stop

d) Brake hard

23. What should you do before stopping?
a) Sound the horn
b) Use the mirrors
c) Select a higher gear
d) Flash your headlights

24. You're following a large vehicle. Why should you stay a safe distance behind it?
a) You'll be able to corner more quickly
b) You'll help the large vehicle to stop more easily
c) You'll allow the driver to see you in their mirrors
d) You'll keep out of the wind better

25. When you see a hazard ahead, you should use the mirrors. Why is this?
a) Because you'll need to accelerate out of danger
b) To assess how your actions will affect following traffic
c) Because you'll need to brake sharply to a stop
d) To check what's happening on the road ahead

26. You're waiting to turn right at the end of a road. Your view is obstructed by parked vehicles. What should you do?
a) Stop and then move forward slowly and carefully for a clear view
b) Move quickly to where you can see so you only block traffic from one direction
c) Wait for a pedestrian to let you know when it's safe for you to emerge
d) Turn your vehicle around immediately and find another junction to use

27. What may happen if you hang objects from your interior mirror?
a) Your view could be obstructed
b) Your sun visor might get tangled
c) Your radio reception might be affected
d) Your windscreen would mist up

28. You're on a long motorway journey. What should you do if you start to feel sleepy?
a) Play some loud music
b) Stop on the hard shoulder for a rest
c) Drive faster to complete your journey sooner
d) Leave the motorway and stop in a safe place

29. Why should you switch your lights on when it first starts to get dark?
a) To make your dials easier to see
b) So others can see you more easily
c) So that you blend in with other drivers
d) Because the street lights are lit

30. What's most likely to distract you while you're driving?
a) Using a mobile phone
b) Using the windscreen wipers
c) Using the demisters
d) Checking the mirrors

31. When may you use a hand-held mobile phone in your car?
a) When receiving a call
b) When suitably parked
c) When driving at less than 30 mph
d) When driving an automatic vehicle

32. You're driving on a wet road. You have to stop your vehicle in an emergency. What should you do?
a) Apply the handbrake and footbrake together
b) Keep both hands on the steering wheel
c) Select reverse gear
d) Give an arm signal

33. What should you do when moving off from behind a parked car?
a) Give a signal after moving off
b) Check both interior and exterior mirrors
c) Look around after moving off
d) Use the exterior mirrors only

34. Your vehicle is fitted with a hand-held telephone. What should you do to use the phone?
a) Reduce your speed
b) Find a safe place to stop
c) Steer the vehicle with one hand
d) Be particularly careful at junctions

35. You lose your way on a busy road. What's the best action to take?
a) Stop at traffic lights and ask pedestrians
b) Shout to other drivers to ask them the way
c) Turn into a side road, stop and check a map
d) Check a map, and keep going with the traffic flow

36. When do windscreen pillars cause a serious obstruction to your view?
a) When you're driving on a motorway
b) When you're driving on a dual carriageway
c) When you're approaching a one-way street
d) When you're approaching bends and junctions

37. You can't see clearly behind when reversing. What should you do?
a) Open the window to look behind
b) Open the door to look behind
c) Look in the nearside mirror
d) Ask someone to guide you

38. What does the term 'blind spot' mean?
a) An area covered by your right-hand mirror
b) An area not covered by your headlights
c) An area covered by your left-hand mirror
d) An area not visible to the driver

39. What's likely to happen if you use a hands-free phone while you're driving?
a) It will improve your safety
b) It will increase your concentration
c) It will reduce your view
d) It will divert your attention

40. You're turning right onto a dual carriageway. What should you do before emerging?
a) Stop, apply the handbrake and then select a low gear
b) Position your vehicle well to the left of the side road
c) Check that the central reservation is wide enough for your vehicle
d) Make sure that you leave enough room for a vehicle behind

41. You're waiting to emerge from a junction. The windscreen pillar is restricting your view. What should you be particularly aware of?
a) Lorries
b) Buses
c) Motorcyclists
d) Coaches

42. How should you use a satellite navigation system so that it doesn't distract you when you're driving?
a) Turn it off while driving in built-up areas
b) Choose a voice that you find calming
c) Only set the destination when you're lost
d) Stop in a safe place before programming the system

43. At a pelican crossing, what must you do when the amber light is flashing?
a) Stop and wait for the green light
b) Stop and wait for the red light
c) Give way to pedestrians waiting to cross
d) Give way to pedestrians already on the crossing

44. Why should you never wave people across at pedestrian crossings?
a) Another vehicle may be coming
b) They may not be looking
c) It's safer for you to carry on
d) They may not be ready to cross

45. What does 'tailgating' mean?
a) Using the rear door of a hatchback car
b) Reversing into a parking space
c) Following another vehicle too closely
d) Driving with rear fog lights on

46. What's the minimum time gap you should leave when following a vehicle on a wet road?
a) One second
b) Two seconds
c) Three seconds
d) Four seconds

47. A long, heavily laden lorry is taking a long time to overtake you. What should you do?
a) Speed up
b) Slow down
c) Hold your speed
d) Change direction

48. Which vehicle will use a blue flashing beacon?
a) Motorway maintenance
b) Bomb disposal
c) Snow plough
d) Breakdown recovery

49. You're being followed by an ambulance showing flashing blue lights. What should you do?
a) Pull over as soon as it's safe to do so
b) Accelerate hard to get away from it
c) Maintain your speed and course
d) Brake harshly and stop well out into the road

50. What type of emergency vehicle is fitted with a green flashing beacon?
a) Fire engine
b) Road gritter
c) Ambulance
d) Doctor's car

51. Who should obey diamond-shaped traffic signs?
a) Tram drivers
b) Bus drivers
c) Lorry drivers
d) Taxi drivers

52. On a road where trams operate, which of these vehicles will be most at risk from the tram rails?
a) Cars
b) Cycles
c) Buses
d) Lorries

53. What should you use your horn for?
a) To alert others to your presence
b) To allow you right of way
c) To greet other road users
d) To signal your annoyance

54. You're in a one-way street and want to turn right. There are two lanes. Where should you position your vehicle?
a) In the right-hand lane
b) In the left-hand lane
c) In either lane, depending on the traffic
d) Just left of the centre line

55. You wish to turn right ahead. Why should you take up the correct position in good time?
a) To allow other drivers to pull out in front of you
b) To give a better view into the road that you're joining
c) To help other road users know what you intend to do
d) To allow drivers to pass you on the right

56. At which type of crossing are cyclists allowed to ride across with pedestrians?
a) Toucan
b) Puffin
c) Pelican
d) Zebra

57. You're driving at the legal speed limit. A vehicle comes up quickly behind you, flashing its headlights. What should you do?
a) Accelerate to make a gap behind you
b) Touch the brakes sharply to show your brake lights
c) Maintain your speed to prevent the vehicle from overtaking
d) Allow the vehicle to overtake

58. When should you flash your headlights at other road users?
a) When showing that you're giving way
b) When showing that you're about to turn
c) When telling them that you have right of way
d) When letting them know that you're there

59. You're approaching an unmarked crossroads. How should you deal with this type of junction?
a) Accelerate and keep to the middle
b) Slow down and keep to the right
c) Accelerate and look to the left
d) Slow down and look both ways

60. The conditions are good and dry. When should you use the 'two-second rule'?
a) Before restarting the engine after it has stalled
b) When checking your gap from the vehicle in front
c) Before using the 'Mirrors – Signal – Manoeuvre' routine
d) When traffic lights change to green

61. At a puffin crossing, which colour follows the green signal?
a) Steady red
b) Flashing amber
c) Steady amber
d) Flashing green

62. You're in a line of traffic. The driver behind you is following very closely. What action should you take?
a) Ignore the following driver and continue to travel within the speed limit
b) Slow down, gradually increasing the gap between you and the vehicle in front
c) Signal left and wave the following driver past
d) Move over to a position just left of the centre line of the road

63. You're driving on a clear night. There's a steady stream of oncoming traffic. The national speed limit applies. Which lights should you use?
a) Full-beam headlights
b) Sidelights
c) Dipped headlights
d) Fog lights

64. You're driving behind a large goods vehicle. What should you do if it signals left but steers to the right?
a) Slow down and let the vehicle turn
b) Drive on, keeping to the left
c) Overtake on the right of it
d) Hold your speed and sound your horn

65. You're waiting in a traffic queue at night. How can you avoid dazzling drivers behind you?
a) Use the parking brake only
b) Use the footbrake only
c) Use the clutch with the accelerator
d) Use the parking brake with the footbrake

66. You're driving in traffic at the speed limit for the road. What should you do if the driver behind is trying to overtake?
a) Move closer to the car ahead, so the driver behind has no room to overtake
b) Wave the driver behind to overtake when it's safe
c) Keep a steady course and allow the driver behind to overtake
d) Accelerate to get away from the driver behind

67. There's a bus lane on your left. The signs show no times of operation. What does this mean?
a) The lane isn't in operation
b) The lane is only in operation at peak times
c) The lane is in operation 24 hours a day
d) The lane is only in operation in daylight hours

68. What should you do when a person herding sheep asks you to stop?
a) Ignore them as they have no authority
b) Stop and switch off your engine
c) Continue on but drive slowly
d) Try to get past quickly

69. What should you do when you're overtaking a horse and rider?
a) Sound your horn as a warning
b) Go past as quickly as possible
c) Flash your headlights as a warning
d) Go past slowly and carefully

70. You're approaching a zebra crossing. Pedestrians are waiting to cross. What should you do?
a) Give way to the elderly and infirm only
b) Slow down and prepare to stop
c) Use your headlights to indicate they can cross
d) Wave at them to cross the road

71. A vehicle pulls out in front of you at a junction. What should you do?
a) Swerve past it and sound your horn
b) Flash your headlights and drive up close behind
c) Slow down and be ready to stop
d) Accelerate past it immediately

72. You're approaching a red light at a puffin crossing. Pedestrians are on the crossing. When will the red light change?
a) When you start to edge forward onto the crossing
b) When the pedestrians have cleared the crossing
c) When the pedestrians push the button on the far side of the crossing
d) When a driver from the opposite direction reaches the crossing

73. In which conditions should you leave at least a two-second gap between your vehicle and the one in front?
a) Wet
b) Dry
c) Damp
d) Foggy

74. You're driving at night on an unlit road, following another vehicle. What should you do?
a) Flash your headlights
b) Use dipped headlights
c) Switch off your headlights
d) Use full-beam headlights

75. You're driving a slow-moving vehicle on a narrow, winding road. What should you do?
a) Keep well out to stop vehicles overtaking dangerously
b) Wave following vehicles past you if you think they can overtake quickly
c) Pull in when you can, to let following vehicles overtake
d) Give a left signal when it's safe for vehicles to overtake you

76. What can a loose filler cap on your diesel fuel tank cause?
a) It can make the engine difficult to start
b) It can make the roads slippery for other road users
c) It can improve your vehicle's fuel consumption
d) It can increase the level of exhaust emissions

77. After refuelling your vehicle, what should you do to avoid spillage?
a) Check that your tank is only three-quarters full
b) Check that you've used a locking filler cap
c) Check that your fuel gauge is working
d) Check that your filler cap is securely fastened

78. What style of driving causes increased risk to everyone?
a) Considerate
b) Defensive
c) Competitive
d) Responsible

79. What's badly affected if the tyres are under-inflated?
a) Braking
b) Indicating
c) Changing gear
d) Parking

80. When mustn't you sound your vehicle's horn?
a) Between 10.00 pm and 6.00 am in a built-up area
b) At any time in a built-up area
c) Between 11.30 pm and 7.00 am in a built-up area
d) Between 11.30 pm and 6.00 am on any road

81. Why have 'red routes' been introduced in major cities?
a) To raise the speed limits
b) To help the traffic flow
c) To provide better parking
d) To allow lorries to load more freely

82. What's the purpose of road humps, chicanes and narrowings?
a) To separate lanes of traffic
b) To increase traffic speed
c) To allow pedestrians to cross
d) To reduce traffic speed

83. What's the purpose of a catalytic converter?
a) To reduce fuel consumption
b) To reduce the risk of fire
c) To reduce harmful exhaust gases
d) To reduce engine wear

84. It's essential that tyre pressures are checked regularly. When should this be done?
a) After any lengthy journey
b) After travelling at high speed
c) When tyres are hot
d) When tyres are cold

85. When will your vehicle use more fuel?
a) When its tyres are under-inflated
b) When its tyres are of different makes
c) When its tyres are over-inflated
d) When its tyres are new

86. How should you dispose of a used vehicle battery?
a) Bury it in your garden
b) Put it in the dustbin
c) Take it to a local-authority site
d) Leave it on waste land

87. What's most likely to cause high fuel consumption?
a) Poor steering control
b) Accelerating around bends
c) Staying in high gears
d) Harsh braking and accelerating

88. The fluid level in your battery is low. What should you top it up with?
a) Battery acid
b) Distilled water
c) Engine oil
d) Engine coolant

89. You're parked on the road at night. Where must you use parking lights?
a) Where there are continuous white lines in the middle of the road
b) Where the speed limit exceeds 30 mph
c) Where you're facing oncoming traffic
d) Where you're near a bus stop

90. How can you reduce the environmental harm caused by your motor vehicle?
a) Only use it for short journeys
b) Don't service it
c) Drive faster than normal
d) Keep engine revs low

91. What can cause excessive or uneven tyre wear?
a) A faulty gearbox
b) A faulty braking system
c) A faulty electrical system
d) A faulty exhaust system

92. You need to top up your battery. What level should you fill it to?
a) The top of the battery
b) Halfway up the battery
c) Just below the cell plates
d) Just above the cell plates

93. Before starting a journey, it's wise to plan your route. How can you do this?
a) Look at a map
b) Contact your local garage
c) Look in your vehicle handbook
d) Check your vehicle registration document

94. Why is it a good idea to plan your journey to avoid busy times?
a) You'll have an easier journey
b) You'll have a more stressful journey
c) Your journey time will be longer
d) It will cause more traffic congestion

95. You avoid busy times when travelling. How will this affect your journey?
a) You're more likely to be held up
b) Your journey time will be longer
c) You'll travel a much shorter distance
d) You're less likely to be delayed

96. It can be helpful to plan your route before starting a journey. Why should you also plan an alternative route?
a) Your original route may be blocked
b) Your maps may have different scales
c) You may find you have to pay a congestion charge
d) You may get held up by a tractor

97. You're making an appointment and will have to travel a long distance. How should you plan for the journey?
a) Allow plenty of time for the trip
b) Plan to travel at busy times
c) Avoid roads with the national speed limit
d) Prevent other drivers from overtaking

98. What can rapid acceleration and heavy braking lead to?
a) Reduced pollution
b) Increased fuel consumption
c) Reduced exhaust emissions
d) Increased road safety

99. Which of these, if allowed to get low, could cause you to crash?
a) Anti-freeze level
b) Brake fluid level
c) Battery water level
d) Radiator coolant level

100. What can cause excessive or uneven tyre wear?
a) Faults in the gearbox
b) Faults in the engine
c) Faults in the suspension
d) Faults in the exhaust system

101. What's the main cause of brake fade?
a) The brakes overheating
b) Air in the brake fluid
c) Oil on the brakes
d) The brakes out of adjustment

102. What should you do if your anti-lock brakes (ABS) warning light stays on?
a) Check the brake-fluid level
b) Check the footbrake free play
c) Check that the handbrake is released
d) Have the brakes checked immediately

103. It's important to wear suitable shoes when you're driving. Why is this?
a) To prevent wear on the pedals
b) To maintain control of the pedals
c) To enable you to adjust your seat
d) To enable you to walk for assistance if you break down

104. What will reduce the risk of neck injury resulting from a collision?
a) An air-sprung seat
b) Anti-lock brakes
c) A collapsible steering wheel
d) A properly adjusted head restraint

105. You're testing your suspension. You notice that your vehicle keeps bouncing when you press down on the front wing. What does this mean?
a) Worn tyres
b) Tyres under-inflated
c) Steering wheel not located centrally
d) Worn shock absorbers

106. How will a roof rack affect your car's performance?
a) There will be less wind noise
b) The engine will use more oil
c) The car will accelerate faster
d) Fuel consumption will increase

107. Which of these makes your tyres illegal?
a) They were bought second-hand
b) They have a large, deep cut in the side wall
c) They're of different makes
d) They have different tread patterns
108. What's the legal minimum depth of tread for car tyres?
a) 1 mm
b) 1.6 mm
c) 2.5 mm
d) 4 mm

109. You're carrying two 13-year-old children and their parents in your car. Who's responsible for seeing that the children wear seat belts?
a) The children's parents
b) You, the driver
c) The front-seat passenger
d) The children

110. How can drivers help the environment?
a) By accelerating harshly
b) By accelerating gently
c) By using leaded fuel
d) By driving faster

111. How can you avoid wasting fuel?
a) By having your vehicle serviced regularly
b) By revving the engine in the lower gears
c) By keeping an empty roof rack on your vehicle
d) By driving at higher speeds where possible

112. What could you do to reduce the volume of traffic on the roads?
a) Drive in a bus lane
b) Use a car with a smaller engine
c) Walk or cycle on short journeys
d) Travel by car at all times

113. What's most likely to waste fuel?
a) Reducing your speed
b) Driving on motorways
c) Using different brands of fuel
d) Under-inflated tyres

114. What does the law require you to keep in good condition?
a) Gears
b) Transmission
c) Door locks
d) Seat belts

115. Up to how much more fuel will you use by driving at 70 mph, compared with driving at 50 mph?
a) 10%
b) 30%
c) 75%
d) 100%

116. When you use the brakes, your vehicle pulls to one side. What should you do?
a) Increase the pressure in your tyres
b) Have the brakes checked as soon as possible
c) Change gear and pump the brake pedal
d) Use your parking brake at the same time

117. What will happen if your car's wheels are unbalanced?
a) The steering will pull to one side
b) The steering will vibrate
c) The brakes will fail
d) The tyres will deflate

118. Turning the steering wheel while stationary can cause damage to which part of your car?
a) Gearbox
b) Engine
c) Brakes
d) Tyres

119. You have to leave valuables in your car. What's the safest thing to do?
a) Put them in a carrier bag
b) Park near a school entrance
c) Lock them out of sight
d) Park near a bus stop

120. Which of the following may help to deter a thief from stealing your car?
a) Always keeping the headlights on
b) Fitting reflective glass windows
c) Always keeping the interior light on
d) Etching the registration number on the windows

121. Which of the following shouldn't be kept in your vehicle?
a) The car dealer's details
b) The owner's manual
c) The service record
d) The vehicle registration document

122. What should you do when leaving your vehicle parked and unattended?
a) Park near a busy junction
b) Park in a housing estate
c) Lock it and remove the key
d) Leave the left indicator on

123. What will improve fuel consumption?
a) Reducing your speed
b) Rapid acceleration
c) Late and harsh braking
d) Driving in lower gears

124. You service your own vehicle. How should you get rid of the old engine oil?
a) Take it to a local-authority site
b) Pour it down a drain
c) Tip it into a hole in the ground
d) Put it in your dustbin

125. Why do MOT tests include a strict exhaust emission test?
a) To recover the cost of expensive garage equipment
b) To help protect the environment against pollution
c) To discover which fuel supplier is used the most
d) To make sure diesel and petrol engines emit the same fumes

126. How can you reduce the damage your vehicle causes to the environment?
a) Use narrow side streets
b) Brake heavily
c) Use busy routes
d) Anticipate well ahead

127. What will be the result of having your vehicle properly serviced?
a) Reduced insurance premiums
b) Lower vehicle tax
c) Better fuel economy
d) Slower journey times

128. You enter a road where there are road humps. What should you do?
a) Maintain a reduced speed throughout
b) Accelerate quickly between each one
c) Always keep to the maximum legal speed
d) Drive slowly at school times only

129. When should you especially check the engine oil level?
a) Before a long journey
b) When the engine is hot
c) Early in the morning
d) Every 6000 miles

130. You're having difficulty finding a parking space in a busy town. You can see there's space on the zigzag lines of a zebra crossing. Can you park there?
a) No, not unless you stay with your car
b) Yes, in order to drop off a passenger
c) Yes, if you don't block people from crossing
d) No, not under any circumstances

131. What should you do when you leave your car unattended for a few minutes?
a) Leave the engine running
b) Switch the engine off but leave the key in
c) Lock it and remove the key
d) Park near a traffic warden

132. When leaving your vehicle, where should you try to park?
a) Opposite a traffic island
b) In a secure car park
c) On a bend
d) At or near a taxi rank

133. Where would parking your vehicle cause an obstruction?
a) Alongside a parking meter
b) In front of a property entrance
c) On your driveway
d) In a marked parking space

134. What's the most important reason for having a properly adjusted head restraint?
a) To make you more comfortable
b) To help you avoid neck injury
c) To help you relax
d) To help you maintain your driving position

135. What causes the most damage to the environment?
a) Choosing a fuel-efficient vehicle
b) Having your vehicle serviced regularly
c) Driving in as high a gear as possible
d) Making a lot of short journeys

136. What can people who live or work in towns and cities do to help reduce urban pollution levels?
a) Drive more quickly
b) Over-rev in a low gear
c) Walk or cycle
d) Drive short journeys

137. How can you reduce the chances of your car being broken into when leaving it unattended?
a) Take all valuables with you
b) Park near a taxi rank
c) Place any valuables on the floor
d) Park near a fire station

138. How can you help to prevent your car radio being stolen?
a) Park in an unlit area
b) Leave the radio turned on
c) Park near a busy junction
d) Install a security-coded radio

139. How can you lessen the risk of your vehicle being broken into at night?
a) Leave it in a well-lit area
b) Park in a quiet side road
c) Don't engage the steering lock
d) Park in a poorly-lit area

140. Which of these will help you to keep your car secure?
a) Vehicle breakdown organisation
b) Vehicle watch scheme
c) Advanced driver's scheme
d) Car maintenance class

141. On a vehicle, where would you find a catalytic converter?
a) In the fuel tank
b) In the air filter
c) On the cooling system
d) On the exhaust system

142. What can driving smoothly achieve?
a) Reduction in journey times by about 15%
b) Increase in fuel consumption by about 15%
c) Reduction in fuel consumption by about 15%
d) Increase in journey times by about 15%

143. Which driving technique can help you save fuel?
a) Using lower gears as often as possible
b) Accelerating sharply in each gear
c) Using each gear in turn
d) Missing out some gears

144. How can driving in an ecosafe manner help protect the environment?
a) Through the legal enforcement of speed regulations
b) By increasing the number of cars on the road
c) Through increased fuel bills
d) By reducing exhaust emissions

145. What does ecosafe driving achieve?
a) Increased fuel consumption
b) Improved road safety
c) Damage to the environment
d) Increased exhaust emissions

146. You're checking your trailer tyres. What's the legal minimum tread depth over the central three-quarters of its breadth?
a) 1 mm
b) 1.6 mm
c) 2 mm
d) 2.6 mm

147. Fuel consumption is at its highest when you're doing what?
a) Braking
b) Coasting
c) Accelerating
d) Steering

148. When is it acceptable for a passenger to travel in a car without wearing wearing a seat belt?
a) When they're under 14 years old
b) When they're under 1.5 metres (5 feet) in height
c) When they're sitting in the rear seat
d) When they're exempt for medical reasons

149. You're driving a friend's children home from school. They're both under 14 years old. Who's responsible for making sure they wear a seat belt or approved child restraint where required?
a) An adult passenger
b) The children
c) You, the driver
d) Your friend

150. You have too much oil in your engine. What could this cause?
a) Low oil pressure
b) Engine overheating
c) Chain wear
d) Oil leaks

151. You're carrying a five-year-old child in the back seat of your car. They're under 1.35 metres (4 feet 5 inches) tall. A correct child restraint isn't available. How should you seat them?
a) Behind the passenger seat
b) Using an adult seat belt
c) Sharing a belt with an adult
d) Between two other children

152. You're carrying an 11-year-old child in the back seat of your car. They're under 1.35 metres (4 feet 5 inches) tall. What must you make sure of?
a) That they sit between two belted people
b) That they can fasten their own seat belt
c) That a suitable child restraint is available
d) That they can see clearly out of the front window

153. You're parked at the side of the road. You'll be waiting some time for a passenger. What should you do?
a) Switch off the engine
b) Apply the steering lock
c) Switch off the radio
d) Use your headlights

154. You want to put a rear-facing baby seat on the front passenger seat, which is protected by a frontal airbag. What must you do before setting off?
a) Deactivate the airbag
b) Turn the seat to face sideways
c) Ask a passenger to hold the baby
d) Put the child in an adult seat belt

155. You're leaving your vehicle parked on a road and unattended. When may you leave the engine running?
a) If you'll be parking for less than five minutes
b) If the battery keeps going flat
c) When parked in a 20 mph zone
d) Never if you're away from the vehicle

156. By how much can stopping distances increase in icy conditions?
a) Two times
b) Three times
c) Five times
d) Ten times

157. In windy conditions, which activity requires extra care?
a) Using the brakes
b) Moving off on a hill
c) Turning into a narrow road
d) Passing pedal cyclists

158. When approaching a right-hand bend, you should keep well to the left. Why is this?
a) To improve your view of the road
b) To overcome the effect of the road's slope
c) To let faster traffic from behind overtake
d) To be positioned safely if you skid

159. You've just gone through deep water. What should you do to make sure your brakes are working properly?
a) Accelerate and keep to a high speed for a short time
b) Go slowly while gently applying the brakes
c) Avoid using the brakes at all for a few miles
d) Stop for at least an hour to allow them time to dry

160. In very hot weather the road surface can become soft. What will this affect?
a) The suspension
b) The exhaust emissions
c) The fuel consumption
d) The tyre grip

161. Where are you most likely to be affected by side winds?
a) On a narrow country lane
b) On an open stretch of road
c) On a busy stretch of road
d) On a long, straight road

162. In good conditions, what's the typical stopping distance at 70 mph?
a) 53 metres (175 feet)
b) 60 metres (197 feet)
c) 73 metres (240 feet)
d) 96 metres (315 feet)

163. What's the shortest overall stopping distance on a dry road at 60 mph?
a) 53 metres (175 feet)
b) 58 metres (190 feet)
c) 73 metres (240 feet)
d) 96 metres (315 feet)

164. You're following a vehicle at a safe distance on a wet road. Another driver overtakes you and pulls into the gap you've left. What should you do?
a) Flash your headlights as a warning
b) Try to overtake safely as soon as you can
c) Drop back to regain a safe distance
d) Stay close to the other vehicle until it moves on

165. You're travelling at 50 mph on a good, dry road. What's your typical overall stopping distance?
a) 36 metres (118 feet)
b) 53 metres (175 feet)
c) 75 metres (245 feet)
d) 96 metres (315 feet)

166. You're on a good, dry road surface. Your brakes and tyres are good. What's the typical overall stopping distance at 40 mph?
a) 23 metres (75 feet)
b) 36 metres (118 feet)
c) 53 metres (175 feet)
d) 96 metres (315 feet)

167. What should you do when overtaking a motorcyclist in strong winds?
a) Pass closely
b) Pass very slowly
c) Pass wide
d) Pass immediately

168. Overall stopping distance is made up of thinking distance and braking distance. You're on a good, dry road surface, with good brakes and tyres. What's the typical braking distance from 50 mph?
a) 14 metres (46 feet)
b) 24 metres (80 feet)
c) 38 metres (125 feet)
d) 55 metres (180 feet)

169. In heavy motorway traffic, the vehicle behind you is following too closely. How can you lower the risk of a collision?
a) Increase your distance from the vehicle in front
b) Brake sharply
c) Switch on your hazard warning lights
d) Move onto the hard shoulder and stop

170. You're following other vehicles in fog. You have your lights on. What else can you do to reduce the chances of being in a collision?
a) Keep close to the vehicle in front
b) Use your main beam instead of dipped headlights
c) Keep up with the faster vehicles
d) Reduce your speed and increase the gap in front

171. You're using a contraflow system. What should you do?
a) Choose an appropriate lane in good time
b) Switch lanes at any time to make progress
c) Increase speed to pass through quickly
d) Follow other motorists closely to avoid long queues

172. You're driving on an icy road. How can you avoid wheelspin?
a) Drive at a slow speed in as high a gear as possible
b) Use the handbrake if the wheels start to slip
c) Brake gently and repeatedly
d) Drive in a low gear at all times

173. What's the main cause of skidding?
a) The weather
b) The driver
c) The vehicle
d) The road

174. You're driving in freezing conditions. What should you do when approaching a sharp bend?
a) Coast into the bend
b) Gently apply your handbrake
c) Firmly use your footbrake
d) Slow down before you reach the bend

175. You're turning left on a slippery road. What should you do if the back of your vehicle slides to the right?
a) Brake firmly and don't turn the steering wheel
b) Steer carefully to the left
c) Steer carefully to the right
d) Brake firmly and steer to the left

176. What should you clear of ice and snow before starting a journey in freezing weather?
a) The aerial
b) The windows
c) The bumper
d) The boot

177. What will help when you're trying to move off on snow?
a) Use the car's lowest gear
b) Use a higher gear than normal
c) Use a high engine speed
d) Use the handbrake and footbrake together

178. What should you do when you're driving in snowy conditions?
a) Brake firmly and quickly
b) Be ready to steer sharply
c) Use sidelights only
d) Brake gently in plenty of time

179. What's the main benefit of driving a four-wheel-drive vehicle?
a) Improved grip on the road
b) Lower fuel consumption
c) Shorter stopping distances
d) Improved passenger comfort

180. You're about to go down a steep hill. What should you do to control the speed of your vehicle?
a) Select a high gear and use the brakes carefully
b) Select a high gear and use the brakes firmly
c) Select a low gear and use the brakes carefully
d) Select a low gear and avoid using the brakes

181. What should you do when parking your vehicle facing downhill?
a) Turn the steering wheel towards the kerb
b) Park close to the bumper of another car
c) Park with two wheels on the kerb
d) Turn the steering wheel away from the kerb

182. You're driving in a built-up area that has traffic-calming measures. What should you do when you approach a road hump?
a) Move across to the left-hand side of the road
b) Wait for any pedestrians to cross
c) Check your mirror and slow down
d) Stop and check both pavements

183. Anti-lock brakes reduce the chances of skidding. When is this particularly important?
a) When you're driving down steep hills
b) When you're braking during normal driving
c) When you're braking in an emergency
d) When you're driving on good road surfaces

184. On what type of road surface may anti-lock brakes not work effectively?
a) Dry
b) Loose
c) Firm
d) Smooth

185. When are anti-lock brakes of most use to you?
a) When you're braking gently
b) When you're braking on rural roads
c) When you're braking harshly
d) When you're braking on a motorway

186. What does driving a vehicle with anti-lock brakes allow you to do?
a) Brake harder because it's impossible to skid
b) Drive at higher speeds
c) Steer and brake harshly at the same time
d) Pay less attention to the road ahead

187. You're driving a vehicle that has anti-lock brakes. How should you apply the footbrake when you need to stop in an emergency?
a) Slowly and gently
b) Slowly but firmly
c) Rapidly and gently
d) Rapidly and firmly

188. In which conditions are your anti-lock brakes most unlikely to prevent skidding?
a) In foggy conditions
b) At night on unlit roads
c) On loose road surfaces
d) On dry tarmac

189. What would suggest you're driving on ice?
a) There's less wind noise
b) There's less tyre noise
c) There's less transmission noise
d) There's less engine noise

190. You're driving along a wet road. How can you tell if your vehicle's tyres are losing their grip on the surface?
a) The engine will stall
b) The steering will feel very heavy
c) The engine noise will increase
d) The steering will feel very light

191. In which conditions will your overall stopping distance increase?
a) In the rain
b) In fog
c) At night
d) In strong winds

192. You're driving on an open road in dry weather. What should the distance be between you and the vehicle in front?
a) A two-second time gap
b) One car length
c) Two metres (6 feet 6 inches)
d) Two car lengths

193. How can you use your vehicle's engine as a brake?
a) By changing to a lower gear
b) By selecting reverse gear
c) By changing to a higher gear
d) By selecting neutral gear

194. When are anti-lock brakes (ABS) most effective?
a) When you keep pumping the foot brake to prevent skidding
b) When you brake normally but grip the steering wheel tightly
c) When you brake promptly and firmly until you've stopped
d) When you apply the handbrake to reduce the stopping distance

195. When will anti-lock brakes take effect?
a) When you don't brake quickly enough
b) When the wheels are about to lock
c) When you haven't seen a hazard ahead
d) When you're speeding on a slippery road surface

196. You're driving on a wet motorway with surface spray. What lights should you use?
a) Hazard warning lights
b) Dipped headlights
c) Rear fog lights
d) Sidelights

197. What can result when you travel for long distances in neutral (known as coasting)?
a) Improvement in control
b) Easier steering
c) Reduction in control
d) Increased fuel consumption

198. What should you do when driving in fog?
a) Use sidelights only
b) Position close to the centre line
c) Allow more time for your journey
d) Keep close to the car in front

199. A driver pulls out of a side road in front of you, causing you to brake hard. What should you do?
a) Ignore the error and stay calm
b) Flash your lights to show your annoyance
c) Sound your horn to show your annoyance
d) Overtake as soon as possible

200. How would age affect an elderly person's driving ability?
a) They won't be able to obtain car insurance
b) They'll need glasses to read road signs
c) They'll take longer to react to hazards
d) They won't signal at junctions

201. You're planning a long journey. Do you need to plan rest stops?
a) Yes, you should plan to stop every half an hour
b) Yes, regular stops help concentration
c) No, you'll be less tired if you get there as soon as possible
d) No, only fuel stops will be needed

202. You're approaching a crossroads. The traffic lights have failed. What should you do?
a) Brake and stop only for large vehicles
b) Brake sharply to a stop before looking
c) Be prepared to brake sharply to a stop
d) Be prepared to stop for any traffic

203. You're following a slower-moving vehicle on a narrow country road. There's a junction just ahead on the right. What should you do?
a) Overtake after checking your mirrors and signalling
b) Only consider overtaking when you're past the junction
c) Accelerate quickly to pass before the junction
d) Slow down and prepare to overtake on the left

204. Why are mirrors often slightly curved (convex)?
a) They give a wider field of vision
b) They totally cover blind spots
c) They make it easier to judge the speed of following traffic
d) They make following traffic look bigger

205. You think the driver of the vehicle in front has forgotten to cancel their right indicator. What should you do?
a) Flash your lights to alert the driver
b) Sound your horn before overtaking
c) Overtake on the left if there's room
d) Stay behind and don't overtake

206. How should you drive in areas with traffic-calming measures?
a) At a reduced speed
b) At the speed limit
c) In the centre of the road
d) With headlights on dipped beam

207. Why are place names painted on the road surface?
a) To restrict the flow of traffic
b) To warn you of oncoming traffic
c) To enable you to change lanes early
d) To prevent you changing lanes

208. Some two-way roads are divided into three lanes. Why are these particularly dangerous?
a) Traffic in both directions can use the middle lane to overtake
b) Traffic can travel faster in poor weather conditions
c) Traffic can overtake on the left
d) Traffic uses the middle lane for emergencies only

209. You're on a dual carriageway. Ahead, you see a vehicle with an amber flashing light. What could this be?
a) An ambulance
b) A fire engine
c) A doctor on call
d) A disabled person's vehicle

210. Where shouldn't you overtake?
a) On a single carriageway
b) On a one-way street
c) Approaching a junction
d) Travelling up a long hill

211. What's an effect of drinking alcohol?
a) Poor judgement of speed
b) A loss of confidence
c) Faster reactions
d) Greater awareness of danger

212. What does the solid white line at the side of the road indicate?
a) Traffic lights ahead
b) Edge of the carriageway
c) Footpath on the left
d) Cycle path

213. Why should the junction on the left be kept clear?
a) To allow vehicles to enter and emerge
b) To allow the bus to reverse
c) To allow vehicles to make a U-turn
d) To allow vehicles to park

214. Your motorway journey is boring and you feel drowsy. What should you do?
a) Stop on the hard shoulder for a sleep
b) Open a window and stop as soon as it's safe and legal
c) Speed up to arrive at your destination sooner
d) Slow down and let other drivers overtake

215. You're turning left at a junction where pedestrians have started to cross. What should you do?
a) Go around them, leaving plenty of room
b) Stop and wave at them to cross
c) Sound your horn and proceed
d) Give way to them

216. You're turning left into a side road. What hazard should you be especially aware of?
a) One-way street
b) Pedestrians
c) Traffic congestion
d) Parked vehicles

217. You intend to turn right into a side road. Why should you check for motorcyclists just before turning?
a) They may be overtaking on your left
b) They may be following you closely
c) They may be emerging from the side road
d) They may be overtaking on your right

218. Why is a toucan crossing different from other crossings?
a) Moped riders can use it
b) It's controlled by a traffic warden
c) It's controlled by two flashing lights
d) Cyclists can use it

219. How will a school crossing patrol signal you to stop?
a) By pointing to children on the opposite pavement
b) By displaying a red light
c) By displaying a 'stop' sign
d) By giving you an arm signal

220. You see a pedestrian carrying a white stick with a red band. What does this tell you?
a) They have limited mobility
b) They're deaf
c) They're blind
d) They're deaf and blind

221. What action would you take when elderly people are crossing the road?
a) Wave them across so they know that you've seen them
b) Be patient and allow them to cross in their own time
c) Rev the engine to let them know that you're waiting
d) Tap the horn in case they're hard of hearing

222. What should you do when you see two elderly pedestrians about to cross the road ahead?
a) Expect them to wait for you to pass
b) Speed up to get past them quickly
c) Stop and wave them across the road
d) Be careful; they may misjudge your speed

223. You're coming up to a roundabout. A cyclist is signalling to turn right. What should you do?
a) Overtake on the right
b) Give a warning with your horn
c) Signal the cyclist to move across
d) Give the cyclist plenty of room

224. Which of these should you allow extra room when overtaking?
a) Lorry
b) Tractor
c) Bicycle
d) Road-sweeping vehicle

225. Why should you look particularly for motorcyclists and cyclists at junctions?
a) They may want to turn into the side road
b) They may slow down to let you turn
c) They're harder to see
d) They might not see you turn

226. You're waiting to come out of a side road. Why should you look carefully for motorcycles?
a) Motorcycles are usually faster than cars
b) Police patrols often use motorcycles
c) Motorcycles can easily be hidden behind obstructions
d) Motorcycles have right of way

227. In daylight, an approaching motorcyclist is using dipped headlights. Why?
a) So that the rider can be seen more easily
b) To stop the battery overcharging
c) To improve the rider's vision
d) The rider is inviting you to proceed

228. Why should motorcyclists wear bright clothing?
a) They must do so by law
b) It helps keep them cool in summer
c) The colours are popular
d) Drivers often do not see them

229. You're unsure what a slow-moving motorcyclist ahead of you is going to do. What should you do?
a) Pass on the left
b) Pass on the right
c) Stay behind
d) Move closer

230. Why will a motorcyclist look round over their right shoulder just before turning right?
a) To listen for following traffic
b) Motorcycles don't have mirrors
c) It helps them balance as they turn
d) To check for traffic in their blind area

231. Which is the most vulnerable road user at road junctions?
a) Car driver
b) Tractor driver
c) Lorry driver
d) Motorcyclist

232. You're approaching a roundabout. There are horses just ahead of you. What should you do?
a) Sound your horn as a warning
b) Treat them like any other vehicle
c) Give them plenty of room
d) Accelerate past as quickly as possible

233. As you approach a pelican crossing, the lights change to green. What should you do if elderly people are halfway across?
a) Wave them to cross as quickly as they can
b) Rev your engine to make them hurry
c) Flash your lights in case they haven't noticed you
d) Wait patiently because they'll probably take longer to cross

234. There are flashing amber lights under a school warning sign. What action should you take?
a) Reduce speed until you're clear of the area
b) Keep up your speed and sound the horn
c) Increase your speed to clear the area quickly
d) Wait at the lights until they change to green

235. You're following two cyclists. They approach a roundabout in the left-hand lane. In which direction should you expect the cyclists to go?
a) Left
b) Right
c) Any direction
d) Straight ahead

236. You're travelling behind a moped. What should you do when you want to turn left just ahead?
a) Overtake the moped before the junction
b) Pull alongside the moped and stay level until just before the junction
c) Sound your horn as a warning and pull in front of the moped
d) Stay behind until the moped has passed the junction

237. You see a horse rider as you approach a roundabout. What should you do if they're signalling right but keeping well to the left?
a) Proceed as normal
b) Keep close to them
c) Cut in front of them
d) Stay well back

238. How would you react to drivers who appear to be inexperienced?
a) Sound your horn to warn them of your presence
b) Be patient and prepare for them to react more slowly
c) Flash your headlights to indicate that it's safe for them to proceed
d) Overtake them as soon as possible

239. What should you do when you're following a learner driver who stalls at a junction?
a) Be patient, as you expect them to make mistakes
b) Stay very close behind and flash your headlights
c) Start to rev your engine if they take too long to restart
d) Immediately steer around them and drive on

240. You're on a country road. What should you expect to see coming towards you on your side of the road?
a) Motorcycles
b) Bicycles
c) Pedestrians
d) Horse riders

241. What should you do when following a car driven by an elderly driver?
a) Expect the driver to drive badly
b) Flash your lights and overtake
c) Be aware that their reactions may be slower than yours
d) Stay very close behind but be careful

242. You're following a cyclist. What should you do when you wish to turn left just ahead?
a) Overtake the cyclist before you reach the junction
b) Pull alongside the cyclist and stay level until after the junction
c) Hold back until the cyclist has passed the junction
d) Go around the cyclist on the junction

243. A horse rider is in the left-hand lane approaching a roundabout. Where should you expect the rider to go?
a) In any direction
b) To the right
c) To the left
d) Straight ahead

244. Powered vehicles used by disabled people are small and hard to see. How do they give early warning when on a dual carriageway?
a) They'll have a flashing red light
b) They'll have a flashing green light
c) They'll have a flashing blue light
d) They'll have a flashing amber light

245. Where should you never overtake a cyclist?
a) Just before you turn left
b) On a left-hand bend
c) On a one-way street
d) On a dual carriageway

246. What does a flashing amber beacon mean when it's on a moving vehicle?
a) The vehicle is slow moving
b) The vehicle has broken down
c) The vehicle is a doctor's car
d) The vehicle belongs to a school crossing patrol

247. You notice horse riders in front. What should you do first?
a) Pull out to the middle of the road
b) Slow down and be ready to stop
c) Accelerate around them
d) Signal right

248. The left-hand pavement is closed due to street repairs. What should you do?
a) Watch out for pedestrians walking in the road
b) Use your right-hand mirror more often
c) Speed up to get past the roadworks more quickly
d) Position close to the left-hand kerb

249. What should you do when you're following a motorcyclist along a road that has a poor surface?
a) Follow closely so they can see you in their mirrors
b) Overtake immediately to avoid delays
c) Allow extra room in case they swerve to avoid potholes
d) Allow the same room as normal to avoid wasting road space

250. You see a pedestrian with a dog wearing a yellow or burgundy coat. What does this indicate?
a) The pedestrian is elderly
b) The pedestrian is a dog trainer
c) The pedestrian is colour-blind
d) The pedestrian is deaf

251. Who may use toucan crossings?
a) Motorcyclists and cyclists
b) Motorcyclists and pedestrians
c) Only cyclists
d) Cyclists and pedestrians

252. Some junctions controlled by traffic lights have a marked area between two stop lines. What's this for?
a) To allow taxis to position in front of other traffic
b) To allow people with disabilities to cross the road
c) To allow cyclists and pedestrians to cross the road together
d) To allow cyclists to position in front of other traffic

253. When you're overtaking a cyclist, you should leave as much room as you would give to a car. What's the main reason for this?
a) The cyclist might speed up
b) The cyclist might get off their bike
c) The cyclist might swerve
d) The cyclist might have to make a left turn

254. What should you do when passing sheep on a road?
a) Briefly sound your horn
b) Go very slowly
c) Pass quickly but quietly
d) Herd them to the side of the road

255. At night, you see a pedestrian wearing reflective clothing and carrying a bright red light. What does this mean?
a) You're approaching roadworks
b) You're approaching an organised walk
c) You're approaching a slow-moving vehicle
d) You're approaching a traffic danger spot

256. You've just passed your test. How can you reduce your risk of being involved in a collision?
a) By always staying close to the vehicle in front
b) By never going over 40 mph
c) By staying in the left-hand lane on all roads
d) By taking further training

257. You want to reverse into a side road, but you aren't sure that the area behind your car is clear. What should you do?
a) Look through the rear window only
b) Get out and check
c) Check the mirrors only
d) Carry on, assuming it's clear

258. You're about to reverse into a side road. A pedestrian is waiting to cross behind you. What should you do?
a) Wave to the pedestrian to stop
b) Give way to the pedestrian
c) Sound your horn to warn the pedestrian
d) Reverse before the pedestrian starts to cross

259. Who's especially in danger of not being seen as you reverse your car?
a) Motorcyclists
b) Car drivers
c) Cyclists
d) Children

260. You want to turn right from a junction but your view is restricted by parked vehicles. What should you do?
a) Move out quickly, but be prepared to stop
b) Sound your horn and pull out if there's no reply
c) Stop, then move forward slowly until you have a clear view
d) Stop, get out and look along the main road to check

261. You're at the front of a queue of traffic waiting to turn right into a side road. Why is it important to check your right mirror just before turning?
a) To look for pedestrians about to cross
b) To check for overtaking vehicles
c) To make sure the side road is clear
d) To check for emerging traffic

262. What must a driver do at a pelican crossing when the amber light is flashing?
a) Signal the pedestrian to cross
b) Always wait for the green light before proceeding
c) Give way to any pedestrians on the crossing
d) Wait for the red-and-amber light before proceeding

263. You've stopped at a pelican crossing. A disabled person is crossing slowly in front of you when the lights change to green. What should you do?
a) Wait for them to finish crossing
b) Drive in front of them
c) Edge forward slowly
d) Sound your horn

264. You're driving past a line of parked cars. You notice a ball bouncing out into the road ahead. What should you do?
a) Continue driving at the same speed and sound your horn
b) Continue driving at the same speed and flash your headlights
c) Slow down and be prepared to stop for children
d) Stop and wave the children across to fetch their ball

265. You want to turn right from a main road into a side road. What should you do just before turning?
a) Cancel your right-turn signal
b) Select first gear
c) Check for traffic overtaking on your right
d) Stop and set the handbrake

266. You're driving in a slow-moving queue of traffic. Just before changing lane, what should you do?
a) Sound the horn and flash your lights
b) Look for motorcyclists filtering through the traffic
c) Give a 'slowing down' arm signal
d) Change down to first gear

267. You're driving in town. There's a bus at the bus stop on the other side of the road. Why should you be careful?
a) The bus might have broken down
b) Pedestrians might come from behind the bus
c) The bus might move off suddenly
d) The bus might remain stationary

268. How should you overtake horse riders?
a) Drive up close and overtake as soon as possible
b) Speed isn't important but allow plenty of room
c) Use your horn just once to warn them
d) Drive slowly and leave plenty of room

269. Why should you allow extra room when overtaking a motorcyclist on a windy day?
a) The rider may turn off suddenly to get out of the wind
b) The rider may be blown across in front of you
c) The rider may stop suddenly
d) The rider may be travelling faster than normal

270. Where should you take particular care to look for motorcyclists and cyclists?
a) On dual carriageways
b) At junctions
c) At zebra crossings
d) On one-way streets

271. You're driving past parked cars. You notice a bicycle wheel sticking out between them. What should you do?
a) Accelerate past quickly and sound your horn
b) Slow down and wave the cyclist across
c) Brake sharply and flash your headlights
d) Slow down and be prepared to stop for a cyclist

272. You're dazzled at night by a vehicle behind you. What should you do?
a) Set your mirror to the anti-dazzle position
b) Set your mirror to dazzle the other driver
c) Brake sharply to a stop
d) Switch your rear lights on and off

273. You're driving towards a zebra crossing. A person in a wheelchair is waiting to cross. What should you do?
a) Continue on your way
b) Wave to the person to cross
c) Wave to the person to wait
d) Be prepared to stop

274. You're waiting to emerge left from a minor road. A large vehicle is approaching from the right. You have time to turn, but you should wait. Why?
a) The large vehicle can easily hide an overtaking vehicle
b) The large vehicle can turn suddenly
c) The large vehicle is difficult to steer in a straight line
d) The large vehicle can easily hide vehicles from the left

275. Before overtaking a large vehicle, you should keep well back. Why is this?
a) To give acceleration space to overtake quickly on blind bends
b) To get the best view of the road ahead
c) To leave a gap in case the vehicle stops and rolls back
d) To offer other drivers a safe gap if they want to overtake you

276. You're travelling behind a bus that pulls up at a bus stop. What should you do?
a) Accelerate past the bus
b) Watch carefully for pedestrians
c) Sound your horn
d) Pull in closely behind the bus

277. You're following a lorry on a wet road. What should you do when spray makes it difficult to see the road ahead?
a) Drop back until you can see better
b) Put your headlights on full beam
c) Keep close to the lorry, away from the spray
d) Speed up and overtake quickly

278. You keep well back while waiting to overtake a large vehicle. What should you do if a car moves into the gap?
a) Sound your horn
b) Drop back further
c) Flash your headlights
d) Start to overtake

279. How should you overtake a long, slow-moving vehicle on a busy road?
a) Follow it closely and keep moving out to see the road ahead
b) Flash your headlights for the oncoming traffic to give way
c) Stay behind until the driver waves you past
d) Keep well back until you can see that it's clear

280. Which of these is least likely to be affected by side winds?
a) Cyclists
b) Motorcyclists
c) High-sided vehicles
d) Cars

281. What's the maximum speed of powered wheelchairs or scooters used by disabled people?
a) 8 mph
b) 12 mph
c) 16 mph
d) 20 mph

282. Why is it more difficult to overtake a large vehicle than a car?
a) It will take longer to pass one
b) It will be fitted with a speed limiter
c) It will have air brakes
d) It will be slow climbing hills

283. It's very windy. You're behind a motorcyclist who's overtaking a high-sided vehicle. What should you do?
a) Overtake the motorcyclist immediately
b) Keep well back
c) Stay level with the motorcyclist
d) Keep close to the motorcyclist

284. You're driving in town. Ahead of you a bus is at a bus stop. Which of the following should you do?
a) Flash your lights to warn the driver of your presence
b) Continue at the same speed but sound your horn as a warning
c) Watch carefully for the sudden appearance of pedestrians
d) Pass the bus as quickly as you possibly can

285. As a driver, why should you be more careful where trams operate?
a) Because they don't have a horn
b) Because they can't stop for cars
c) Because they don't have lights
d) Because they can't steer to avoid you

286. You're towing a caravan. Which is the safest type of rear-view mirror to use?
a) Interior wide-angle mirror
b) Extended-arm side mirrors
c) Ordinary door mirrors
d) Ordinary interior mirror

287. You're driving in heavy traffic on a wet road. Spray makes it difficult to be seen. What lights should you use?
a) Full-beam headlights
b) Sidelights only
c) Rear fog lights if visibility is more than 100 metres (328 feet)
d) Dipped headlights

288. It's a very windy day and you're about to overtake a cyclist. What should you do?
a) Overtake very slowly
b) Keep close as you pass
c) Sound your horn repeatedly
d) Allow extra room

289. When may you overtake another vehicle on the left?
a) When you're in a one-way street
b) When approaching a motorway slip road where you'll be turning off
c) When the vehicle in front is signalling to turn left
d) When a slower vehicle is travelling in the right-hand lane of a dual carriageway

290. You're travelling in very heavy rain. How is this likely to affect your overall stopping distance?
a) It will be doubled
b) It will be halved
c) It will be ten times greater
d) It will be no different

291. What should you do when you're overtaking at night?
a) Wait until a bend so that you can see oncoming headlights
b) Sound your horn twice before moving out
c) Put your headlights on full beam
d) Beware of bends in the road ahead

292. When may you wait in a box junction?
a) When you're stationary in a queue of traffic
b) When approaching a pelican crossing
c) When approaching a zebra crossing
d) When oncoming traffic prevents you turning right

293. What do traffic-calming measures do?
a) Stop road rage
b) Make overtaking easier
c) Slow traffic down
d) Make parking easier

294. You're on a motorway in fog. The left-hand edge of the motorway can be identified by reflective studs. What colour are they?
a) Green
b) Amber
c) Red
d) White

295. What's a rumble device designed to do?
a) Give directions
b) Prevent cattle escaping
c) Alert you to low tyre pressure
d) Alert you to a hazard

296. What should you do when making a journey in foggy conditions?
a) Follow other vehicles' tail lights closely
b) Avoid using dipped headlights
c) Leave plenty of time for your journey
d) Keep two seconds behind the vehicle ahead

297. What must you do when overtaking a car at night?
a) Flash your headlights before overtaking
b) Select a higher gear
c) Switch your lights to full beam before overtaking
d) Make sure you don't dazzle other road users

298. You're travelling on a road that has speed humps. What should you do when the driver in front is travelling more slowly than you?
a) Sound your horn
b) Overtake as soon as you can
c) Flash your headlights
d) Slow down and stay behind

299. How would you identify a section of road used by trams?
a) There would be metal studs around it
b) There would be zigzag markings alongside it
c) There would be a different surface texture
d) There would be yellow hatch markings around it

300. What should you do when you meet an oncoming vehicle on a single-track road?
a) Reverse back to the main road
b) Carry out an emergency stop
c) Stop at a passing place
d) Switch on your hazard warning lights

301. The road is wet. Why might a motorcyclist steer round drain covers on a bend?
a) To avoid puncturing the tyres on the edge of the drain covers
b) To prevent the motorcycle sliding on the metal drain covers
c) To help judge the bend using the drain covers as marker points
d) To avoid splashing pedestrians on the pavement

302. Why should you always reduce your speed when travelling in fog?
a) The brakes don't work as well
b) You'll be dazzled by other headlights
c) The engine will take longer to warm up
d) It's more difficult to see what's ahead

303. How will your vehicle be affected when you drive up steep hills?
a) The higher gears will pull better
b) The steering will feel heavier
c) Overtaking will be easier
d) The engine will work harder

304. You're driving on the motorway in windy conditions. What should you do as you pass a high-sided vehicle?
a) Increase your speed
b) Be wary of a sudden gust
c) Drive alongside very closely
d) Expect normal conditions

305. What should you do to correct a rear-wheel skid?
a) Not steer at all
b) Steer away from it
c) Steer into it
d) Apply your handbrake

306. You're driving in fog. Why should you keep well back from the vehicle in front?
a) In case it changes direction suddenly
b) In case its fog lights dazzle you
c) In case it stops suddenly
d) In case its brake lights dazzle you

307. What should you do if you park on the road when it's foggy?
a) Leave sidelights switched on
b) Leave dipped headlights and fog lights switched on
c) Leave dipped headlights switched on
d) Leave main-beam headlights switched on

308. You're driving at night and are dazzled by vehicle headlights coming towards you. What should you do?
a) Pull down your sun visor
b) Slow down or stop
c) Flash your main-beam headlights
d) Shade your eyes with your hand

309. When may front fog lights be used?
a) When visibility is seriously reduced
b) When they're fitted above the bumper
c) When they aren't as bright as the headlights
d) When an audible warning device is used

310. You're driving with your front fog lights switched on. Earlier fog has now cleared. What should you do?
a) Leave them on if other drivers have their lights on
b) Switch them off as long as visibility remains good
c) Flash them to warn oncoming traffic that it's foggy
d) Drive with them on instead of your headlights

311. Why should you switch off your rear fog lights when the fog has cleared?
a) To allow your headlights to work
b) To stop draining the battery
c) To stop the engine losing power
d) To prevent dazzling following drivers

312. What will happen if you use rear fog lights in good conditions?
a) They'll make it safer when towing a trailer
b) They'll protect you from larger vehicles
c) They'll dazzle other drivers
d) They'll make following drivers keep back

313. What can fitting chains to your wheels help to prevent?
a) Damage to the road surface
b) Wear to the tyres
c) Skidding in deep snow
d) The brakes locking

314. How can you use your vehicle's engine to control your speed?
a) By changing to a lower gear
b) By selecting reverse gear
c) By changing to a higher gear
d) By selecting neutral

315. Why could it be dangerous to keep the clutch down, or select neutral, for long periods of time while you're driving?
a) Fuel spillage will occur
b) Engine damage may be caused
c) You'll have less steering and braking control
d) It will wear tyres out more quickly

316. You're driving on an icy road. What distance from the car in front should you drive?
a) Four times the normal distance
b) Six times the normal distance
c) Eight times the normal distance
d) Ten times the normal distance

317. You're driving on a well-lit motorway on a clear night. What must you do?
a) Use only your sidelights
b) Use your headlights
c) Use rear fog lights
d) Use front fog lights

318. You're on a motorway at night, with other vehicles just ahead of you. Which lights should you have on?
a) Front fog lights
b) Main-beam headlights
c) Sidelights only
d) Dipped headlights

319. What will affect your vehicle's stopping distance?
a) The speed limit
b) The street lighting
c) The time of day
d) The condition of the tyres

320. You're driving on a motorway at night. When may you switch off your headlights?
a) When there are vehicles close in front of you
b) When you're travelling below 50 mph
c) When the motorway is lit
d) When your vehicle is broken down on the hard shoulder

321. When will you feel the effects of engine braking?
a) When you only use the handbrake
b) When you're in neutral
c) When you change to a lower gear
d) When you change to a higher gear

322. Daytime visibility is poor but not seriously reduced. Which lights should you switch on?
a) Headlights and fog lights
b) Front fog lights
c) Dipped headlights
d) Rear fog lights

323. Why are vehicles fitted with rear fog lights?
a) To make them more visible when driving at high speed
b) To show when they've broken down in a dangerous position
c) To make them more visible in thick fog
d) To warn drivers following closely to drop back

324. While you're driving in fog, it becomes necessary to use front fog lights. What should you remember?
a) Only use them in heavy traffic conditions
b) Don't use them on motorways
c) Only use them on dual carriageways
d) Switch them off when visibility improves

325. What should you do when there's been a heavy fall of snow?
a) Drive with your hazard warning lights on
b) Don't drive unless you have a mobile phone
c) Only drive when your journey is short
d) Don't drive unless it's essential

326. You're driving down a long, steep hill. You suddenly notice that your brakes aren't working as well as normal. What's the usual cause of this?
a) The brakes overheating
b) Air in the brake fluid
c) Oil on the brakes
d) Badly adjusted brakes

327. You have to make a journey in fog. What should you do before you set out?
a) Top up the radiator with anti-freeze
b) Make sure that you have a warning triangle in the vehicle
c) Make sure that the windows are clean
d) Check the battery

328. You've just driven out of fog. What must you do now that visibility has improved?
a) Switch off your fog lights
b) Keep your rear fog lights switched on
c) Keep your front fog lights switched on
d) Leave your fog lights switched on in case the fog returns

329. Why is it dangerous to leave rear fog lights on when they're not needed?
a) They may be confused with brake lights
b) The bulbs would fail
c) Electrical systems could be overloaded
d) Direction indicators may not work properly

330. What will happen if you hold the clutch pedal down or roll in neutral for too long?
a) It will use more fuel
b) It will cause the engine to overheat
c) It will reduce your control
d) It will improve tyre wear

331. You're driving down a steep hill. Why could it be dangerous to keep the clutch down or roll in neutral for too long?
a) Fuel consumption will be higher
b) Your vehicle will pick up speed
c) It will damage the engine
d) It will wear tyres out more quickly

332. Why is it bad technique to coast when driving downhill?
a) The fuel consumption will increase
b) The engine will overheat
c) The tyres will wear more quickly
d) The vehicle will gain speed

333. Why is travelling in neutral for long distances (known as coasting) wrong?
a) It will cause the car to skid
b) It will make the engine stall
c) The engine will run faster
d) There won't be any engine braking

334. When must you use dipped headlights during the day?
a) All the time
b) On narrow streets
c) In poor visibility
d) When parking

335. You're braking on a wet road. Your vehicle begins to skid. It doesn't have anti-lock brakes. What's the first thing you should do?
a) Quickly pull up the handbrake
b) Release the footbrake
c) Push harder on the brake pedal
d) Gently use the accelerator

336. What should you do when you're joining a motorway?
a) Use the hard shoulder
b) Stop at the end of the acceleration lane
c) Slow to a stop before joining the motorway
d) Give way to traffic already on the motorway

337. What's the national speed limit on motorways for cars and motorcycles?
a) 30 mph
b) 50 mph
c) 60 mph
d) 70 mph

338. Which vehicles should use the left-hand lane on a three-lane motorway?
a) Any vehicle
b) Large vehicles only
c) Emergency vehicles only
d) Slow vehicles only

339. Which of these isn't allowed to travel in the right-hand lane of a three-lane motorway?
a) A small delivery van
b) A motorcycle
c) A vehicle towing a trailer
d) A motorcycle and sidecar

340. You break down on a motorway. You need to call for help. Why may it be better to use an emergency roadside telephone rather than a mobile phone?
a) It connects you to a local garage
b) Using a mobile phone will distract other drivers
c) It allows easy location by the emergency services
d) Mobile phones don't work on motorways

341. You've had a breakdown on the hard shoulder of a motorway. When the problem has been fixed, how should you rejoin the main carriageway?
a) Move out onto the carriageway, then build up your speed
b) Move out onto the carriageway using your hazard warning lights
c) Gain speed on the hard shoulder before moving out onto the carriageway
d) Wait on the hard shoulder until someone flashes their headlights at you

342. You're travelling along a motorway. Where would you find a crawler or climbing lane?
a) On a steep gradient
b) Before a service area
c) Before a junction
d) Along the hard shoulder

343. On which part of a motorway are amber reflective studs found?
a) Between the hard shoulder and the carriageway
b) Between the acceleration lane and the carriageway
c) Between the central reservation and the carriageway
d) Between each pair of lanes

344. What colour are the reflective studs between the lanes on a motorway?
a) Green
b) Amber
c) White
d) Red

345. What colour are the reflective studs between a motorway and its slip road?
a) Amber
b) White
c) Green
d) Red

346. You've broken down on a motorway. In which direction should you walk to find the nearest emergency telephone?
a) With the traffic flow
b) Facing oncoming traffic
c) In the direction shown on the marker posts
d) In the direction of the nearest exit

347. You're joining a motorway. Why is it important to make full use of the slip road?
a) Because there is space available to turn round if you need to
b) To allow you direct access to the overtaking lanes
c) To build up a speed similar to traffic on the motorway
d) Because you can continue on the hard shoulder

348. How should you use the emergency telephone on a motorway?
a) Stay close to the carriageway
b) Face the oncoming traffic
c) Keep your back to the traffic
d) Stand on the hard shoulder

349. You're on a motorway. What colour are the reflective studs on the left of the carriageway?
a) Green
b) Red
c) White
d) Amber

350. On a three-lane motorway, which lane should you normally use?
a) Left
b) Right
c) Centre
d) Either the right or centre

351. What should you do when going through a contraflow system on a motorway?
a) Ensure that you don't exceed 30 mph
b) Keep a good distance from the vehicle ahead
c) Switch lanes to keep the traffic flowing
d) Stay close to the vehicle ahead to reduce queues

352. You're on a three-lane motorway. There are red reflective studs on your left and white ones to your right. Which lane are you in?
a) In the right-hand lane
b) In the middle lane
c) On the hard shoulder
d) In the left-hand lane

353. You're approaching roadworks on a motorway. What should you do?
a) Speed up to clear the area quickly
b) Always use the hard shoulder
c) Obey all speed limits
d) Stay very close to the vehicle in front

354. Which vehicles are prohibited from using the motorway?
a) Powered mobility scooters
b) Motorcycles over 50 cc
c) Double-deck buses
d) Cars with automatic transmission

355. What should you do when driving or riding along a motorway?
a) Look much further ahead than you would on other roads
b) Travel much faster than you would on other roads
c) Maintain a shorter separation distance than you would on other roads
d) Concentrate more than you would on other roads

356. What should you do immediately after joining a motorway?
a) Try to overtake
b) Re-adjust your mirrors
c) Position your vehicle in the centre lane
d) Keep in the left-hand lane

357. What's the right-hand lane used for on a three-lane motorway?
a) Emergency vehicles only
b) Overtaking
c) Vehicles towing trailers
d) Coaches only

358. What should you use the hard shoulder of a motorway for?
a) Stopping in an emergency
b) Leaving the motorway
c) Stopping when you're tired
d) Joining the motorway

359. When are you allowed to stop on a motorway?
a) When you need to walk and get fresh air
b) When you wish to pick up hitchhikers
c) When you're signalled to do so by flashing red lights
d) When you need to use a mobile telephone

360. You're travelling in the left-hand lane of a three-lane motorway. How should you react to traffic joining from a slip road?
a) Race the other vehicles
b) Move to another lane
c) Maintain a steady speed
d) Switch on your hazard warning lights

361. What basic rule applies when you're using a motorway?
a) Use the lane that has the least traffic
b) Keep to the left-hand lane unless overtaking
c) Overtake on the side that's clearest
d) Try to keep above 50 mph to prevent congestion

362. You're travelling along a motorway. When are you allowed to overtake on the left?
a) When you can see well ahead that the hard shoulder is clear
b) When the traffic in the right-hand lane is signalling right
c) When you warn drivers behind by signalling left
d) When in queues and traffic to your right is moving more slowly than you are

363. On a motorway, what's an emergency refuge area used for?
a) In cases of emergency or breakdown
b) If you think you'll be involved in a road rage incident
c) For a police patrol to park and watch traffic
d) For construction and road workers to store emergency equipment

364. Traffic officers operate on motorways and some primary routes in England. What are they authorised to do?
a) Stop and arrest drivers who break the law
b) Repair broken-down vehicles on the motorway
c) Issue fixed penalty notices
d) Stop and direct anyone on a motorway

365. You're on a motorway. A red cross is displayed above the hard shoulder. What does this mean?
a) Pull up in this lane to answer your mobile phone
b) Use this lane as a running lane
c) This lane can be used if you need a rest
d) You shouldn't travel in this lane

366. You're on a smart motorway. A mandatory speed limit is displayed above the hard shoulder. What does this mean?
a) You shouldn't travel in this lane
b) The hard shoulder can be used as a running lane
c) You can park on the hard shoulder if you feel tired
d) You can pull up in this lane to answer a mobile phone

367. What's the aim of a smart motorway?
a) To prevent overtaking
b) To reduce rest stops
c) To prevent tailgating
d) To reduce congestion

368. You're using a smart motorway. What happens when it's operating?
a) Speed limits above lanes are advisory
b) The national speed limit will apply
c) The speed limit is always 30 mph
d) You must obey the speed limits shown

369. Why can it be an advantage for traffic speed to stay constant over a longer distance?
a) You'll do more stop–start driving
b) You'll use far more fuel
c) You'll be able to use more direct routes
d) Your overall journey time will normally improve

370. You shouldn't normally travel on the hard shoulder of a motorway. When can you use it?
a) When taking the next exit
b) When traffic is stopped
c) When signs direct you to
d) When traffic is slow moving

371. What's used to reduce traffic bunching on a motorway?
a) Variable speed limits
b) Contraflow systems
c) National speed limits
d) Lane closures

372. When may you stop on a motorway?
a) If you have to read a map
b) When you're tired and need a rest
c) If your mobile phone rings
d) In an emergency or breakdown

373. Unless signs show otherwise, what's the national speed limit for a car or motorcycle on a motorway?
a) 50 mph
b) 60 mph
c) 70 mph
d) 80 mph

374. You're on a motorway and there are red flashing lights above every lane. What must you do?
a) Pull onto the hard shoulder
b) Slow down and watch for further signals
c) Leave at the next exit
d) Stop and wait

375. You're on a three-lane motorway. A red cross is showing above the hard shoulder and mandatory speed limits above all other lanes. What does this mean?
a) The hard shoulder can be used as a rest area if you feel tired
b) The hard shoulder is for emergency or breakdown use only
c) The hard shoulder can be used as a normal running lane
d) The hard shoulder has a speed limit of 50 mph

376. You're travelling along a motorway and feel tired. Where should you stop to rest?
a) On the hard shoulder
b) At the nearest service area
c) On a slip road
d) On the central reservation

377. You're towing a trailer on a motorway. What's the speed limit for a car towing a trailer on this road?
a) 40 mph
b) 50 mph
c) 60 mph
d) 70 mph

378. What should the left-hand lane of a motorway be used for?
a) Breakdowns and emergencies only
b) Overtaking slower traffic in the other lanes
c) Slow vehicles only
d) Normal driving

379. You're driving on a motorway and have to slow down quickly due to a hazard ahead. How can you warn drivers behind of the hazard?
a) Switch on your hazard warning lights
b) Switch on your headlights
c) Sound your horn
d) Flash your headlights

380. Your car gets a puncture while you're driving on the motorway. You get it onto the hard shoulder. What should you do?
a) Carefully change the wheel yourself
b) Use an emergency telephone and call for help
c) Try to wave down another vehicle for help
d) Only change the wheel if you have a passenger to help you

381. You're driving on a motorway. By mistake, you go past the exit that you wanted to take. What should you do?
a) Carefully reverse on the hard shoulder
b) Carry on to the next exit
c) Carefully reverse in the left-hand lane
d) Make a U-turn at a gap in the central reservation

382. Your vehicle has broken down on a motorway. You aren't able to stop on the hard shoulder. What should you do?
a) Switch on your hazard warning lights
b) Stop following traffic and ask for help
c) Attempt to repair your vehicle quickly
d) Stand behind your vehicle to warn others

383. Why is it particularly important to carry out a check on your vehicle before making a long motorway journey?
a) You'll have to do more harsh braking on motorways
b) Motorway service stations don't deal with breakdowns
c) The road surface will wear down the tyres faster
d) Continuous high speeds increase the risk of your vehicle breaking down

384. You're driving on a motorway. The car in front shows its hazard warning lights for a short time. What does this tell you?
a) The driver wants you to overtake
b) The other car is going to change lanes
c) Traffic ahead is slowing or stopping suddenly
d) There's a police speed check ahead

385. You're driving on the motorway. Well before you reach your intended exit, where should you position your vehicle?
a) In the middle lane
b) In the left-hand lane
c) On the hard shoulder
d) In any lane

386. What restrictions apply to new drivers holding a provisional driving licence?
a) They can't drive over 30 mph
b) They can't drive at night
c) They can't drive unaccompanied
d) They can't drive with more than one passenger

387. Your vehicle breaks down on the hard shoulder of a motorway. You need to use your mobile phone to call for help. What should you do?
a) Stand at the rear of the vehicle while making the call
b) Phone a friend and ask them to come and collect you
c) Open the bonnet to help the emergency services know you've broken down
d) Check your location from the marker posts on the left

388. You're towing a trailer along a three-lane motorway. When may you use the right-hand lane?
a) When there are lane closures
b) When there's slow-moving traffic
c) When you can maintain a high speed
d) When large vehicles are in the left and centre lanes

389. You're on a motorway. There's a contraflow system ahead. What would you expect to find?
a) Temporary traffic lights
b) Lower speed limits
c) Wider lanes than normal
d) Speed humps

390. When may you stop on the hard shoulder of a motorway?
a) In an emergency
b) If you feel tired and need to rest
c) If you miss the exit that you wanted
d) To pick up a hitchhiker

391. What's the national speed limit for cars and motorcycles on a dual carriageway?
a) 30 mph
b) 50 mph
c) 60 mph
d) 70 mph

392. There are no speed-limit signs on the road. How is a 30 mph limit indicated?
a) By hazard warning lines
b) By street lighting
c) By pedestrian islands
d) By double or single yellow lines

393. You see street lights but no speed-limit signs. What will the speed limit usually be?
a) 30 mph
b) 40 mph
c) 50 mph
d) 60 mph

394. There's a tractor ahead. You want to overtake but you aren't sure whether it's safe. What should you do?
a) Follow another vehicle as it overtakes the tractor
b) Sound your horn to make the tractor pull over
c) Speed past, flashing your lights at oncoming traffic
d) Stay behind the tractor if you're in any doubt

395. Which vehicle is most likely to take an unusual course at a roundabout?
a) Estate car
b) Milk float
c) Delivery van
d) Long lorry

396. When mustn't you stop on a clearway?
a) At any time
b) When it's busy
c) In the rush hour
d) During daylight hours

397. When can you park on the right-hand side of a road at night?
a) When you're in a one-way street
b) When you have your sidelights on
c) When you're more than 10 metres (32 feet) from a junction
d) When you're under a lamppost

398. On a three-lane dual carriageway, what can the right-hand lane be used for?
a) Overtaking only, never turning right
b) Overtaking or turning right
c) Fast-moving traffic only
d) Turning right only, never overtaking

399. You're approaching a busy junction. What should you do when, at the last moment, you realise you're in the wrong lane?
a) Continue in that lane
b) Force your way across
c) Stop until the area has cleared
d) Use clear arm signals to cut across

400. Where may you overtake on a one-way street?
a) Only on the left-hand side
b) Overtaking isn't allowed
c) Only on the right-hand side
d) On either the right or the left

401. How should you signal when going straight ahead at a roundabout?
a) Indicate left before leaving the roundabout
b) Don't indicate at any time
c) Indicate right when approaching the roundabout
d) Indicate left when approaching the roundabout

402. Which vehicle might have to take a different course from normal at roundabouts?
a) Sports car
b) Van
c) Estate car
d) Long vehicle

403. On which occasion may you enter a box junction?
a) When there are fewer than two vehicles ahead
b) When signalled by another road user
c) When your exit road is clear
d) When traffic signs direct you

404. When may you stop and wait in a box junction?
a) When oncoming traffic prevents you from turning right
b) When you're in a queue of traffic turning left
c) When you're in a queue of traffic going ahead
d) When you're on a roundabout

405. Which person's signal to stop must you obey?
a) A motorcyclist
b) A pedestrian
c) A police officer
d) A bus driver

406. You see a pedestrian waiting at a zebra crossing. What should you normally do?
a) Go on quickly before they step onto the crossing
b) Stop before you reach the zigzag lines and let them cross
c) Stop to let them cross and wait patiently
d) Ignore them as they're still on the pavement

407. Who can use a toucan crossing?
a) Cars and motorcycles
b) Cyclists and pedestrians
c) Buses and lorries
d) Trams and trains

408. You're waiting at a pelican crossing. What does it mean when the red light changes to flashing amber?
a) Wait for pedestrians on the crossing to clear
b) Move off immediately without any hesitation
c) Wait for the green light before moving off
d) Get ready and go when the continuous amber light shows

409. You're turning right at a crossroads. An oncoming driver is also turning right. What's the advantage of turning behind the oncoming vehicle?
a) You'll have a clearer view of any approaching traffic
b) You'll use less fuel because you can stay in a higher gear
c) You'll have more time to turn
d) You'll be able to turn without stopping

410. You're travelling along a street with parked vehicles on the left-hand side. Why should you keep your speed down?
a) So that oncoming traffic can see you more clearly
b) You may set off car alarms
c) There may be delivery lorries on the street
d) Children may run out from between the vehicles

411. What should you do when you meet an obstruction on your side of the road?
a) Carry on, as you have priority
b) Give way to oncoming traffic
c) Wave oncoming vehicles through
d) Accelerate to get past first

412. You're on a two-lane dual carriageway. Why would you use the right-hand lane?
a) To overtake slower traffic
b) For normal progress
c) When staying at the minimum allowed speed
d) To keep driving at a constant high speed

413. Who has priority at an unmarked crossroads?
a) The larger vehicle
b) No-one has priority
c) The faster vehicle
d) The smaller vehicle

414. What's the nearest you may park to a junction?
a) 10 metres (32 feet)
b) 12 metres (39 feet)
c) 15 metres (49 feet)
d) 20 metres (66 feet)

415. Where shouldn't you park?
a) On a road with a 40 mph speed limit
b) At or near a bus stop
c) Where there's no pavement
d) Within 20 metres (65 feet) of a junction

416. You're waiting at a level crossing. A train passes but the lights keep flashing. What must you do?
a) Carry on waiting
b) Phone the signal operator
c) Edge over the stop line and look for trains
d) Park and investigate

417. What must you do when entering roadworks where a temporary speed limit is displayed?
a) Obey the speed limit
b) Obey the limit, but only during rush hour
c) Ignore the displayed limit
d) Use your own judgment; the limit is only advisory

418. You're on a well-lit road at night, in a built-up area. How will using dipped headlights help?
a) You can see further along the road
b) You can go at a much faster speed
c) You can switch to main beam quickly
d) You can be easily seen by others

419. The dual carriageway you're turning right onto has a very narrow central reservation. What should you do?
a) Proceed to the central reservation and wait
b) Wait until the road is clear in both directions
c) Stop in the first lane so that other vehicles give way
d) Emerge slightly to show your intentions

420. What's the national speed limit on a single carriageway road for cars and motorcycles?
a) 30 mph
b) 50 mph
c) 60 mph
d) 70 mph

421. You park at night on a road with a 40 mph speed limit. What should you do?
a) Park facing the traffic
b) Park with parking lights on
c) Park with dipped headlights on
d) Park near a street light

422. You're travelling on a motorway in England. You must stop when signalled to do so by which of these?
a) Flashing amber lights above your lane
b) A traffic officer
c) Pedestrians on the hard shoulder
d) A driver who has broken down

423. You're going straight ahead at a roundabout. How should you signal?
a) Signal right on the approach and then left to leave the roundabout
b) Signal left after you leave the roundabout and enter the new road
c) Signal right on the approach to the roundabout and keep the signal on
d) Signal left just after you pass the exit before the one you're going to take

424. When may you drive over a footpath?
a) To overtake slow-moving traffic
b) When the pavement is very wide
c) If there are no pedestrians nearby
d) To get onto a property

425. What's the speed limit for a car towing a small caravan along a dual carriageway?
a) 50 mph
b) 40 mph
c) 70 mph
d) 60 mph

426. A cycle lane, marked by a solid white line, is in operation. What does this mean for car drivers?
a) The lane may be used for parking your car
b) You may drive in the lane at any time
c) The lane may be used when necessary
d) You mustn't drive in that lane

427. You intend to turn left from a main road into a minor road. What should you do as you approach it?
a) Keep just left of the middle of the road
b) Keep in the middle of the road
c) Swing out to the right just before turning
d) Keep well to the left of the road

428. You're waiting at a level crossing. The red warning lights continue to flash after a train has passed by. What should you do?
a) Get out and investigate
b) Telephone the signal operator
c) Continue to wait
d) Drive across carefully

429. You're driving over a level crossing. The warning lights come on and a bell rings. What should you do?
a) Get everyone out of the vehicle immediately
b) Stop and reverse back to clear the crossing
c) Keep going and clear the crossing
d) Stop immediately and use your hazard warning lights

430. You're on a busy main road and find that you're travelling in the wrong direction. What should you do?
a) Turn into a side road on the right and reverse into the main road
b) Make a U-turn in the main road
c) Make a 'three-point' turn in the main road
d) Turn around in a side road

431. During which manoeuvre may you remove your seat belt?
a) Reversing
b) Hill start
c) Emergency stop
d) Driving slowly

432. Over what distance are you allowed to reverse?
a) No further than is necessary
b) No more than a car's length
c) As far as it takes to reverse around a corner
d) The length of a residential street

433. What should you do when you're unsure whether it's safe to reverse your vehicle?
a) Sound your horn
b) Rev your engine
c) Get out and check
d) Reverse slowly

434. When may you reverse from a side road into a main road?
a) Only if both roads are clear of traffic
b) Not at any time
c) At any time
d) Only if the main road is clear of traffic

435. You want to turn right at a box junction. There's oncoming traffic. What should you do?
a) Wait in the box junction if your exit is clear
b) Wait before the junction until it's clear of all traffic
c) Drive on; you can't turn right at a box junction
d) Drive slowly into the box junction when signalled by oncoming traffic

436. You're reversing your vehicle into a side road. When would the greatest hazard to passing traffic occur?
a) After you've completed the manoeuvre
b) Just before you actually begin to manoeuvre
c) After you've entered the side road
d) When the front of your vehicle swings out

437. Where's the safest place to park your vehicle at night?
a) In a garage
b) On a busy road
c) In a quiet car park
d) Near a red route

438. When may you stop on an urban clearway?
a) To set down and pick up passengers
b) To use a mobile telephone
c) To ask for directions
d) To load or unload goods

439. You're looking for somewhere to park your vehicle. The area is full except for spaces marked 'disabled use'. What can you do?
a) You can use these spaces when elsewhere is full
b) You can park in one of these spaces if you stay with your vehicle
c) You can use one of the spaces as long as one is kept free
d) You can't park there, unless you're permitted to do so

440. You're on a road that's only wide enough for one vehicle. A car is coming towards you. What should you do?
a) Pull into a passing place on your right
b) Force the other driver to reverse
c) Pull into a passing place if your vehicle is wider
d) Pull into a passing place on your left

441. You're driving at night with your headlights on full beam. A vehicle is overtaking you. When should you dip your lights?
a) Some time after the vehicle has passed you
b) Before the vehicle starts to pass you
c) Only if the other driver dips their headlights
d) As soon as the vehicle passes you

442. Other than direction indicators, how can you give signals to other road users?
a) By using brake lights
b) By using sidelights
c) By using fog lights
d) By using interior lights

443. You're parked in a busy high street. What's the safest way to turn your vehicle around so you can go the opposite way?
a) Find a quiet side road to turn around in
b) Drive into a side road and reverse into the main road
c) Get someone to stop the traffic
d) Do a U-turn

444. To help keep your vehicle secure at night, where should you park?
a) Near a police station
b) In a quiet road
c) On a red route
d) In a well-lit area

445. You're driving in the right-hand lane of a dual carriageway. You see signs showing that the right-hand lane is closed 800 yards ahead. What should you do?
a) Keep in that lane until you reach the queue
b) Move to the left immediately
c) Wait and see which lane is moving faster
d) Move to the left in good time

446. You're driving on a road that has a cycle lane. The lane is marked by a broken white line. What does this mean?
a) You shouldn't drive in the lane unless it's unavoidable
b) There's a reduced speed limit for motor vehicles using the lane
c) Cyclists can travel in both directions in that lane
d) The lane must be used by motorcyclists in heavy traffic

447. What must you have to park in a disabled car space?
a) A Blue Badge
b) A wheelchair
c) An advanced driver certificate
d) An adapted vehicle

448. When must you stop your vehicle?
a) If you're involved in an incident that causes damage or injury
b) At a junction where there are 'give way' lines
c) At the end of a one-way street
d) Before merging onto a motorway

449. How can you identify traffic signs that give orders?
a) They're rectangular with a yellow border
b) They're triangular with a blue border
c) They're square with a brown border
d) They're circular with a red border

450. For how long is an MOT certificate normally valid?
a) Three years after the date it was issued
b) 10,000 miles
c) One year after the date it was issued
d) 30,000 miles

451. What is a cover note?
a) A document issued before you receive your driving licence
b) A document issued before you receive your insurance certificate
c) A document issued before you receive your registration document
d) A document issued before you receive your MOT certificate

452. You've just passed your practical test. You don't hold a full licence in another category. Within two years you get six penalty points on your licence. What will you have to do?
a) Retake only your theory test
b) Retake your theory and practical tests
c) Retake only your practical test
d) Reapply for your full licence immediately

453. For how long is a Statutory Off-Road Notification (SORN) valid?
a) Until the vehicle is taxed, sold or scrapped
b) Until the vehicle is insured and MOT'd
c) Until the vehicle is repaired or modified
d) Until the vehicle is used on the road

454. What is a Statutory Off-Road Notification (SORN)?
a) A notification to tell DVSA that a vehicle doesn't have a current MOT
b) Information kept by the police about the owner of a vehicle
c) A notification to tell DVLA that a vehicle isn't being used on the road
d) Information held by insurance companies to check a vehicle is insured

455. What's the maximum fine for driving without insurance?
a) Unlimited
b) £500
c) £1000
d) £5000

456. Who's legally responsible for ensuring that a vehicle registration certificate (V5C) is updated?
a) The registered vehicle keeper
b) The vehicle manufacturer
c) Your insurance company
d) The licensing authority

457. In which of these circumstances must you show your insurance certificate?
a) When making a SORN
b) When buying or selling a vehicle
c) When a police officer asks you for it
d) When having an MOT inspection

458. Which of these is needed before you can legally use a vehicle on the road?
a) A valid driving licence
b) Breakdown cover
c) Proof of your identity
d) A vehicle handbook

459. What must you have when you apply to renew your vehicle tax?
a) Valid insurance
b) The vehicle's chassis number
c) The handbook
d) A valid driving licence

460. A police officer asks to see your documents. You don't have them with you. Within what time must you produce them at a police station?
a) 5 days
b) 7 days
c) 14 days
d) 21 days

461. What must you make sure of before you drive someone else's vehicle?
a) That the vehicle owner has third-party insurance cover
b) That your own vehicle has insurance cover
c) That the vehicle is insured for your use
d) That the insurance documents are in the vehicle

462. Your car needs to pass an MOT test. What may be invalidated if you drive the car without a current MOT certificate?
a) The vehicle service record
b) Your insurance
c) The vehicle tax
d) Your vehicle registration document

463. What must a newly qualified driver do?
a) Display green L plates
b) Keep under 40 mph for 12 months
c) Be accompanied on a motorway
d) Have valid motor insurance

464. You have third-party insurance. What does this cover?
a) Damage to your vehicle
b) Fire damage to your vehicle
c) Flood damage to your vehicle
d) Damage to other vehicles

465. Who's responsible for paying the vehicle tax?
a) The driver of the vehicle
b) The registered keeper of the vehicle
c) The car dealer
d) The Driver and Vehicle Licensing Agency (DVLA)

466. What information is found on a vehicle registration document?
a) The registered keeper
b) The type of insurance cover
c) The service history details
d) The date of the MOT

467. When must you contact the vehicle licensing authority?
a) When you take your vehicle abroad on holiday
b) When you change your vehicle
c) When you use your vehicle for work
d) When your vehicle's insurance is due

468. When must you notify the licensing authority?
a) When your health affects your driving
b) When you have to work abroad
c) When you lend your vehicle to someone
d) When your vehicle needs an MOT certificate

469. When may the cost of your insurance come down?
a) When you're under 25 years old
b) When you don't wear glasses
c) When you pass the driving test first time
d) When you complete the Pass Plus scheme

470. Which of these is a requirement before you can supervise a learner driver?
a) You must have held a licence for at least a year
b) You must be at least 21 years old
c) You must be an approved driving instructor
d) You must hold an advanced driving certificate

471. Your car requires an MOT certificate. When is it legal to drive it without an MOT certificate?
a) Up to seven days after the old certificate has run out
b) When driving to an MOT centre to arrange an appointment
c) When driving the car with the owner's permission
d) When driving to an appointment at an MOT centre

472. A new car will need its first MOT test when it's how old?
a) One year
b) Three years
c) Five years
d) Seven years

473. The Pass Plus scheme has been created for new drivers. What's its main purpose?
a) To allow you to drive faster
b) To allow you to carry passengers
c) To improve your basic skills
d) To let you drive on motorways

474. Your vehicle is insured third-party only. What does this cover?
a) Damage to your vehicle
b) Damage to other vehicles
c) Injury to yourself
d) All damage and injury

475. What's the legal minimum insurance cover you must have to drive on public roads?
a) Third party, fire and theft
b) Comprehensive
c) Third party only
d) Personal injury cover

476. You claim on your insurance to have your car repaired. Your policy has an excess of £100. What does this mean?
a) The insurance company will pay the first £100 of any claim
b) You'll be paid £100 if you don't claim within one year
c) Your vehicle is insured for a value of £100 if it's stolen
d) You'll have to pay the first £100 of the cost of repairs to your car

477. What's the purpose of the Pass Plus scheme?
a) To give you a discount on your MOT
b) To improve your basic driving skills
c) To increase your mechanical knowledge
d) To allow you to drive anyone else's vehicle

478. What does the Pass Plus scheme enable newly qualified drivers to do?
a) Widen their driving experience
b) Supervise a learner driver
c) Increase their insurance premiums
d) Avoid mechanical breakdowns

479. You see a car on the hard shoulder of a motorway with a 'help' pennant displayed. What does this mean?
a) The driver is likely to be a disabled person
b) The driver is first-aid trained
c) The driver is a foreign visitor
d) The driver is a rescue patrol officer

480. When should you use hazard warning lights?
a) When you slow down quickly on a motorway because of a hazard ahead
b) When you leave your car at the roadside to visit a shop
c) When you wish to stop on double yellow lines
d) When you need to park on the pavement

481. When are you allowed to use hazard warning lights?
a) When stopped and temporarily obstructing traffic
b) When travelling during darkness without headlights
c) When parked on double yellow lines to visit a shop
d) When travelling slowly because you're lost

482. You're going through a congested tunnel and have to stop. What should you do?
a) Pull up very close to the vehicle in front to save space
b) Ignore any message signs, as they're never up to date
c) Keep a safe distance from the vehicle in front
d) Make a U-turn and find another route

483. On a motorway, when should the hard shoulder be used?
a) When answering a mobile phone
b) When an emergency arises
c) When taking a short rest
d) When checking a road map

484. You arrive at the scene of a crash where someone is bleeding heavily from a wound in their arm. Nothing is embedded in the wound. What could you do to help?
a) Walk them around and keep them talking
b) Dab the wound
c) Get them a drink
d) Apply pressure over the wound

485. You're at an incident. What could you do to help a casualty who's unconscious?
a) Take photographs of the scene
b) Check that they're breathing normally
c) Move them to somewhere more comfortable
d) Splash their face with cool water

486. Following a collision, someone has suffered a burn. The burn needs to be cooled. What's the shortest time it should be cooled for?
a) 5 minutes
b) 10 minutes
c) 15 minutes
d) 20 minutes

487. A casualty isn't breathing normally and needs CPR. At what rate should you press down and release on the centre of their chest?
a) 10 times per minute
b) 120 times per minute
c) 60 times per minute
d) 240 times per minute

488. A person has been injured. They may be suffering from shock. What are the warning signs to look for?
a) Flushed complexion
b) Warm dry skin
c) Slow pulse
d) Pale grey skin

489. An injured person has been placed in the recovery position. They're unconscious but breathing normally. What else should be done?
a) Press firmly between their shoulders
b) Place their arms by their side
c) Give them a hot sweet drink
d) Check their airway remains open

490. An injured motorcyclist is lying unconscious in the road. The traffic has stopped and there's no further danger. What should you do to help?
a) Remove their safety helmet
b) Seek medical assistance
c) Move the person off the road
d) Remove their leather jacket

491. What should you do if you see a large box fall from a lorry onto the motorway?
a) Go to the next emergency telephone and report the hazard
b) Catch up with the lorry and try to get the driver's attention
c) Stop close to the box until the police arrive
d) Pull over to the hard shoulder, then remove the box

492. You're going through a long tunnel. What will warn you of congestion or an incident ahead?
a) Hazard warning lines
b) Other drivers flashing their lights
c) Variable message signs
d) Areas with hatch markings

493. An adult casualty isn't breathing. To maintain circulation, CPR should be given. What's the correct depth to press down on their chest?
a) 1 to 2 centimetres
b) 5 to 6 centimetres
c) 10 to 15 centimetres
d) 15 to 20 centimetres

494. You're the first to arrive at the scene of a crash. What should you do?
a) Leave as soon as another motorist arrives
b) Flag down other motorists to help you
c) Drag all casualties away from the vehicles
d) Call the emergency services promptly

495. You're the first person to arrive at an incident where people are badly injured. You've switched on your hazard warning lights and checked all engines are stopped. What else should you do?
a) Make sure that an ambulance is called for
b) Stop other cars and ask the drivers for help
c) Try and get people who are injured to drink something
d) Move the people who are injured clear of their vehicles

496. You arrive at the scene of a motorcycle crash. The rider is injured. When should their helmet be removed?
a) Only when it's essential
b) Always straight away
c) Only when the motorcyclist asks
d) Always, unless they're in shock

497. You arrive at an incident. There's no danger from fire or further collisions. What's your first priority when attending to an unconscious motorcyclist?
a) Check whether they're breathing normally
b) Check whether they're bleeding
c) Check whether they have any broken bones
d) Check whether they have any bruising

498. At an incident, someone is unconscious. What would your priority be?
a) Find out their name
b) Wake them up
c) Make them comfortable
d) Check their airway is open

499. You've stopped at an incident to give help. What should you do?
a) Keep injured people warm and comfortable
b) Give injured people something to eat
c) Keep injured people on the move by walking them around
d) Give injured people a warm drink

500. There's been a collision. A driver is suffering from shock. What should you do?
a) Give them a drink
b) Reassure them
c) Ask who caused the incident
d) Offer them a cigarette

501. You arrive at the scene of a motorcycle crash. No other vehicle is involved. The rider is unconscious and lying in the middle of the road. What's the first thing you should do at the scene?
a) Move the rider out of the road
b) Warn other traffic
c) Clear the road of debris
d) Give the rider reassurance

502. At an incident, a small child isn't breathing. What should you do to try and help?
a) Find their parents and get permission to help
b) Open their airway and begin CPR
c) Put them in the recovery position and slap their back
d) Talk to them confidently until an ambulance arrives

503. At an incident, a casualty isn't breathing. What should you do while helping them to start breathing again?
a) Put their arms across their chest
b) Shake them firmly
c) Roll them onto their side
d) Tilt their head back gently

504. At an incident, someone is suffering from severe burns. What should you do to help them?
a) Apply lotions to the injury
b) Burst any blisters
c) Remove anything sticking to the burns
d) Douse the burns with clean, cool water

505. You arrive at an incident. A pedestrian is bleeding heavily from a leg wound. The leg isn't broken and there's nothing in the wound. How could you help?
a) Dab the wound to stop the bleeding
b) Keep the casualty's legs flat on the ground
c) Fetch them a warm drink
d) Apply firm pressure over the wound

506. At an incident, a casualty is unconscious but breathing. When should you move them?
a) When an ambulance is on its way
b) When bystanders advise you to
c) When there's further danger
d) When bystanders will help you

507. At an incident, it's important to look after any casualties. What should you do with them when the area is safe?
a) Move them away from the vehicles
b) Ask them how it happened
c) Give them something to eat
d) Keep them where they are

508. You're involved in a collision. Afterwards, which document may the police ask you to produce?
a) Vehicle registration document
b) Driving licence
c) Theory test certificate
d) Vehicle service record

509. After a collision, someone is unconscious in their vehicle. When should you call the emergency services?
a) Only as a last resort
b) As soon as possible
c) After you've woken them up
d) After checking for broken bones

510. A collision has just happened. An injured person is lying in a busy road. What's the first thing you should do to help?
a) Treat the person for shock
b) Warn other traffic
c) Place them in the recovery position
d) Make sure the injured person is kept warm

511. At an incident, what should you do with a casualty who has stopped breathing?
a) Keep their head tilted forwards as far as possible
b) Follow the DR ABC code
c) Raise their legs to help with circulation
d) Try to give them something to drink

512. You're at the scene of an incident. Someone is suffering from shock. How should you treat them?
a) Reassure them confidently
b) Offer them a cigarette
c) Give them a warm drink
d) Offer them some food

513. There's been a collision. A motorcyclist is lying injured and unconscious. Unless it's essential, why should you not usually attempt to remove their helmet?
a) They might not want you to
b) This could result in more serious injury
c) They'll get too cold if you do this
d) You could scratch the helmet

514. You've broken down on a two-way road. You have a warning triangle. At least how far from your vehicle should you place the warning triangle?
a) 5 metres (16 feet)
b) 25 metres (82 feet)
c) 45 metres (147 feet)
d) 100 metres (328 feet)

515. You break down on a level crossing. The lights haven't yet begun to flash. What's the first thing you should do?
a) Tell drivers behind what has happened
b) Leave your vehicle and get everyone clear
c) Walk down the track and signal the next train
d) Stay in your car until you're told to move

516. Your tyre bursts while you're driving. What should you do?
a) Pull on the handbrake
b) Brake as quickly as possible
c) Pull up slowly at the side of the road
d) Continue on at a normal speed

517. Your vehicle has a puncture on a motorway. What should you do?
a) Drive slowly to the next service area to get assistance
b) Pull up on the hard shoulder. Change the wheel as quickly as possible
c) Pull up on the hard shoulder. Use the emergency phone to get assistance
d) Switch on your hazard warning lights. Stop in your lane

518. You've stalled in the middle of a level crossing and can't restart the engine. The warning bells start to ring. What should you do?
a) Get out of the car and clear of the crossing
b) Run down the track to warn the signal operator
c) Carry on trying to restart the engine
d) Push the vehicle clear of the crossing

519. You're driving on a motorway. When can you use hazard warning lights?
a) When a vehicle is following too closely
b) When you slow down quickly because of danger ahead
c) When you're towing another vehicle
d) When you're driving on the hard shoulder

520. You've broken down on a motorway. When you use the emergency telephone, what will you be asked for?
a) Details about your vehicle
b) Your driving licence details
c) The name of your vehicle's insurance company
d) Your employer's details

521. Before driving through a tunnel, what should you do?
a) Switch off your radio
b) Remove any sunglasses
c) Close your sunroof
d) Switch on your windscreen wipers

522. You're driving through a tunnel and the traffic is flowing normally. What should you do?
a) Use parking lights
b) Use front spotlights
c) Use dipped headlights
d) Use rear fog lights

523. What safeguard could you take against fire risk to your vehicle?
a) Keep water levels above maximum
b) Check out any strong smell of fuel
c) Avoid driving with a full tank of fuel
d) Use fuel additives

524. You're on the motorway. Luggage falls from your vehicle. What should you do?
a) Stop at the next emergency telephone and contact the police
b) Stop on the motorway and switch on hazard warning lights while you pick it up
c) Walk back up the motorway to pick it up
d) Pull up on the hard shoulder and wave traffic down

525. While you're driving, a warning light on your vehicle's instrument panel comes on. What should you do?
a) Continue if the engine sounds all right
b) Hope that it's just a temporary electrical fault
c) Deal with the problem when there's more time
d) Check out the problem quickly and safely

526. Your vehicle breaks down in a tunnel. What should you do?
a) Stay in your vehicle and wait for the police
b) Stand in the lane behind your vehicle to warn others
c) Stand in front of your vehicle to warn oncoming drivers
d) Switch on hazard warning lights, then go and call for help

527. Your vehicle catches fire while driving through a tunnel. It's still drivable. What should you do?
a) Leave it where it is, with the engine running
b) Pull up, then walk to an emergency telephone
c) Park it away from the carriageway
d) Drive it out of the tunnel if you can do so

528. You're in a tunnel. Your vehicle is on fire and you can't drive it. What should you do?
a) Stay in the vehicle and close the windows
b) Switch on hazard warning lights
c) Leave the engine running
d) Switch off all of your lights

529. What should you do as you approach a long road tunnel?
a) Put on your sunglasses and use the sun visor
b) Turn your headlights on to main beam
c) Change down to a lower gear
d) Make sure your radio is tuned to the frequency shown

530. Your vehicle has broken down on an automatic railway level crossing. What should you do first?
a) Get everyone out of the vehicle and clear of the crossing
b) Telephone your vehicle recovery service to move it
c) Walk along the track to give warning to any approaching trains
d) Try to push the vehicle clear of the crossing as soon as possible

531. What should you carry for use in the event of a collision?
a) Road map
b) Can of petrol
c) Jump leads
d) Fire extinguisher

532. You have a collision while your car is moving. What's the first thing you must do?
a) Stop only if someone waves at you
b) Call the emergency services
c) Stop at the scene of the incident
d) Call your insurance company

533. You're in collision with another moving vehicle. Someone is injured and your vehicle is damaged. What information should you find out?
a) Whether the other driver is licensed to drive
b) The other driver's name, address and telephone number
c) The destination of the other driver
d) The occupation of the other driver

534. You lose control of your car and damage a garden wall. No-one is around. What must you do?
a) Report the incident to the police within 24 hours
b) Go back to tell the house owner the next day
c) Report the incident to your insurance company when you get home
d) Find someone in the area to tell them about it immediately

535. You're towing a small trailer on a busy three-lane motorway. What must you do if all the lanes are open?
a) Not exceed 50 mph
b) Not overtake
c) Have a stabiliser fitted
d) Use only the left-hand and centre lanes

536. What should you do if a trailer starts to swing from side to side while you're towing it?
a) Ease off the accelerator to reduce your speed
b) Let go of the steering wheel and let it correct itself
c) Brake hard and hold the pedal down
d) Accelerate until it stabilises

537. On which occasion should you inflate your tyres to more than their normal pressure?
a) When the roads are slippery
b) When the vehicle is fitted with anti-lock brakes
c) When the tyre tread is worn below 2 mm
d) When carrying a heavy load

538. How will a heavy load on your roof rack affect your vehicle's handling?
a) It will improve the road holding
b) It will reduce the stopping distance
c) It will make the steering lighter
d) It will reduce stability

539. What can be badly affected when you overload your vehicle?
a) The vehicle's gearbox
b) The vehicle's ventilation
c) The vehicle's handling
d) The vehicle's battery

540. Who's responsible for making sure that a vehicle isn't overloaded?
a) The driver of the vehicle
b) The owner of the items being carried
c) The person who loaded the vehicle
d) The licensing authority

541. You're planning to tow a caravan. Which of these will be the biggest aid to the vehicle handling?
a) A jockey wheel fitted to the towbar
b) Power steering fitted to the towing vehicle
c) Anti-lock brakes fitted to the towing vehicle
d) A stabiliser fitted to the towbar

542. Are passengers allowed to ride in a caravan that's being towed?
a) Yes, if they're over 14
b) No, not at any time
c) Only if all the seats in the towing vehicle are full
d) Only if a stabiliser is fitted

543. A trailer must stay securely hitched to the towing vehicle. What additional safety device must be fitted to a trailer braking system?
a) Stabiliser
b) Jockey wheel
c) Corner steadies
d) Breakaway cable

544. You wish to tow a trailer. Where would you find the maximum noseweight allowed on your vehicle's tow hitch?
a) In the vehicle handbook
b) In The Highway Code
c) In your vehicle registration certificate
d) In your licence documents

545. How should a load be carried on your roof rack?
a) Securely fastened with suitable restraints
b) Loaded towards the rear of the vehicle
c) Visible in your exterior mirror
d) Covered with plastic sheeting

546. You're carrying a child in your car. They're under three years old. Which of these is a suitable restraint?
a) A child seat
b) An adult holding a child
c) An adult seat belt
d) An adult lap belt

Answers

1. A	24. C	47. B
2. C	25. B	48. B
3. A	26. A	49. A
4. C	27. A	50. D
5. B	28. D	51. A
6. D	29. B	52. B
7. B	30. A	53. A
8. B	31. B	54. A
9. C	32. B	55. C
10. C	33. B	56. A
11. B	34. B	57. D
12. B	35. C	58. D
13. B	36. D	59. D
14. D	37. D	60. B
15. C	38. D	61. C
16. D	39. D	62. B
17. C	40. C	63. C
18. A	41. C	64. A
19. C	42. D	65. A
20. D	43. D	66. C
21. C	44. A	67. C
22. C	45. C	68. B
23. B	46. D	69. D

70. B	94. A	118. D
71. C	95. D	119. C
72. B	96. A	120. D
73. B	97. A	121. D
74. B	98. B	122. C
75. C	99. B	123. A
76. B	100. C	124. A
77. D	101. A	125. B
78. C	102. D	126. D
79. A	103. B	127. C
80. C	104. D	128. A
81. B	105. D	129. A
82. D	106. D	130. D
83. C	107. B	131. C
84. D	108. B	132. B
85. A	109. B	133. B
86. C	110. B	134. B
87. D	111. A	135. D
88. B	112. C	136. C
89. B	113. D	137. A
90. D	114. D	138. D
91. B	115. B	139. A
92. D	116. B	140. B
93. A	117. B	141. D

142. C	166. B	190. D
143. D	167. C	191. A
144. D	168. C	192. A
145. B	169. A	193. A
146. B	170. D	194. C
147. C	171. A	195. B
148. D	172. A	196. B
149. C	173. B	197. C
150. D	174. D	198. C
151. B	175. C	199. A
152. C	176. B	200. C
153. A	177. B	201. B
154. A	178. D	202. D
155. D	179. A	203. B
156. D	180. C	204. A
157. D	181. A	205. D
158. A	182. C	206. A
159. B	183. C	207. C
160. D	184. B	208. A
161. B	185. C	209. D
162. D	186. C	210. C
163. C	187. D	211. A
164. C	188. C	212. B
165. B	189. B	213. A

214. B	238. B	262. C
215. D	239. A	263. A
216. B	240. C	264. C
217. D	241. C	265. C
218. D	242. C	266. B
219. C	243. A	267. B
220. D	244. D	268. D
221. B	245. A	269. B
222. D	246. A	270. B
223. D	247. B	271. D
224. C	248. A	272. A
225. C	249. C	273. D
226. C	250. D	274. A
227. A	251. D	275. B
228. D	252. D	276. B
229. C	253. C	277. A
230. D	254. B	278. B
231. D	255. B	279. D
232. C	256. D	280. D
233. D	257. B	281. A
234. A	258. B	282. A
235. C	259. D	283. B
236. D	260. C	284. C
237. D	261. B	285. D

286. B	310. B	334. C
287. D	311. D	335. B
288. D	312. C	336. D
289. A	313. C	337. D
290. A	314. A	338. A
291. D	315. C	339. C
292. D	316. D	340. C
293. C	317. B	341. C
294. C	318. D	342. A
295. D	319. D	343. C
296. C	320. D	344. C
297. D	321. C	345. C
298. D	322. C	346. C
299. C	323. C	347. C
300. C	324. D	348. B
301. B	325. D	349. B
302. D	326. A	350. A
303. D	327. C	351. B
304. B	328. A	352. D
305. C	329. A	353. C
306. C	330. C	354. A
307. A	331. B	355. A
308. B	332. D	356. D
309. A	333. D	357. B

358. A	382. A	406. C
359. C	383. D	407. B
360. B	384. C	408. A
361. B	385. B	409. A
362. D	386. C	410. D
363. A	387. D	411. B
364. D	388. A	412. A
365. D	389. B	413. B
366. B	390. A	414. A
367. D	391. D	415. B
368. D	392. B	416. A
369. D	393. A	417. A
370. C	394. D	418. D
371. A	395. D	419. B
372. D	396. A	420. C
373. C	397. A	421. B
374. D	398. B	422. B
375. B	399. A	423. D
376. B	400. D	424. D
377. C	401. A	425. D
378. D	402. D	426. D
379. A	403. C	427. D
380. B	404. A	428. C
381. B	405. C	429. C

430. D	454. C	478. A
431. A	455. A	479. A
432. A	456. A	480. A
433. C	457. C	481. A
434. B	458. A	482. C
435. A	459. A	483. B
436. D	460. B	484. D
437. A	461. C	485. B
438. A	462. B	486. B
439. D	463. D	487. B
440. D	464. D	488. D
441. D	465. B	489. D
442. A	466. A	490. B
443. A	467. B	491. A
444. D	468. A	492. C
445. D	469. D	493. B
446. A	470. B	494. D
447. A	471. D	495. A
448. A	472. B	496. A
449. D	473. C	497. A
450. C	474. B	498. D
451. B	475. C	499. A
452. B	476. D	500. B
453. A	477. B	501. B

502. B	518. A	534. A
503. D	519. B	535. D
504. D	520. A	536. A
505. D	521. B	537. D
506. C	522. C	538. D
507. D	523. B	539. C
508. B	524. A	540. A
509. B	525. D	541. D
510. B	526. D	542. B
511. B	527. D	543. D
512. A	528. B	544. A
513. B	529. D	545. A
514. C	530. A	546. A
515. B	531. D	
516. C	532. C	
517. C	533. B	

Explanations

1. A toucan crossing is designed to allow pedestrians and cyclists to cross at the same time. Look out for cyclists approaching the crossing at speed.

2. Emergency vehicles may have either a blue, orange or green flashing beacon. Emergency doctor's cars will display a green flashing beacon

3. Coasting is when you allow the vehicle to freewheel in neutral or with the clutch pedal depressed. Speed will increase as you lose the benefits of engine braking and have less control. You shouldn't coast, especially when approaching hazards such as junctions or bends and when travelling downhill.

4. Riders of two-wheeled vehicles are particularly vulnerable. When you overtake them, allow plenty of room. Always check to the left as you pass.

5. Bus-lane signs show the vehicles allowed to use the lane and also its times of operation. Where no times are shown, the bus lane is in operation 24 hours a day.

6. These signs apply only to tram drivers, but you should know their meaning so that you're aware of the priorities and are able to anticipate the actions of the driver.

7. The legal tread depth of 1.6 mm applies to the central three-quarters of a tyre's breadth, over its entire circumference.

8. Driving at a higher speed increases your fuel usage. Driving at 70 mph as opposed to 50 mph increases this fuel usage by about 10%

9. Top up the battery with distilled water and make sure each cell plate is covered.

10. Note that this is the typical stopping distance. It will take at least this distance to think, brake and stop in good conditions. In poor conditions, it will take much longer.

11. A broken-down vehicle in a tunnel can cause serious congestion and danger to other road users. If your vehicle breaks down, get help without delay. Switch on your hazard warning lights, then go to an emergency telephone to call for help.

12. A mandatory speed-limit sign above the hard shoulder shows that this part of the road can be used as a running lane between junctions. You must stay within the speed limit. Look out for vehicles that may have broken down and could be blocking the hard shoulder.

13. You must stop if you've been involved in a collision which results in injury or damage. The police may ask to see your driving licence and insurance details at the time or later at a police station.

14. Have your eyesight tested before you start your practical training. Then, throughout your driving life, have checks periodically, as your vision may change.

15. Knowing the colours of the reflective studs on the road will help you judge your position, especially at night, in foggy conditions or when visibility is poor.

16. On a motorway, all traffic should use the left-hand lane unless overtaking. When overtaking a number of slower vehicles, move back to the left-hand lane when you're safely past. Check your mirrors frequently and don't stay in the middle or right-hand lane if the left-hand lane is free.

17. Large, slow-moving vehicles can hinder the progress of other traffic. On a steep gradient, an extra crawler lane may be provided for slow-moving vehicles to allow faster-moving traffic to flow more easily.

18. You won't be able to drive on a motorway alone until you've passed your driving test

19. If you have to make a U-turn, slow down and ensure that the road is clear in both directions. Make sure that the road is wide enough for you to carry out the manoeuvre safely.

20. As you begin to think about overtaking, ask yourself whether it's really necessary. If you can't see well ahead, stay back and wait for a safer place to pull out.

21. It's illegal to use a hand-held mobile or similar device when driving or riding, except in a genuine emergency. The safest option is to switch off your mobile phone before you set off, and use a message service. If you've forgotten to switch your phone off and it rings, you should ignore it. When you've stopped in a safe place, you can see who called and return the call if necessary.

22. The longer traffic lights have been on green, the sooner they'll change. Allow for this as you approach traffic lights that you know have been on green for a while. They're likely to change soon, so you should be prepared to stop.

23. Before pulling up, check the mirrors to see what's happening behind you. Also assess what's ahead and make sure you give the correct signal if it will help other road users.

24. If you're following a large vehicle but are so close to it that you can't see its exterior mirrors, the driver won't be able to see you. Keeping well back will also allow you to see the road ahead by looking past on either side of the large vehicle.

25. You should be constantly scanning the road for clues about what's going to happen next. Check your mirrors regularly, particularly as soon as you spot a hazard. What's happening behind may affect your response to hazards ahead.

26. At junctions, your view is often restricted by buildings, trees or parked cars. You need to be able to see in order to judge a safe gap. Edge forward slowly and keep looking all the time. Don't cause other road users to change speed or direction as you emerge.

27. Ensure that you can see clearly through the windscreen of your vehicle. Stickers or hanging objects could obstruct your view or draw your attention away from the road.

28. If you feel sleepy, you should leave the motorway at a service area or at the next exit and stop in a safe place to rest. A supply of fresh air can help to keep you alert before you reach the exit, but it isn't a substitute for stopping and resting.

29. Your headlights and tail lights help others on the road to see you. It may be necessary to turn on your lights during the day if visibility is reduced; for example, due to heavy rain. In these conditions, the light might fade before the street lights are timed to switch on. Be seen to be safe.

30. It's easy to be distracted. Planning your journey before you set off is important. A few sensible precautions are to tune your radio to stations in your area of travel, take planned breaks, and plan your route. Except for emergencies, it's illegal to use a hand-held mobile phone while driving. Even using a hands-free kit can severely distract your attention.

31. It's illegal to use a hand-held mobile phone while driving, except in a genuine emergency. Even using a hands-free kit can distract your attention. Park in a safe and convenient place before receiving or making a call or using text messaging. Then you'll also be free to take notes or refer to papers.

32. As you drive, look well ahead and all around so that you're ready for any hazards that might develop. If you have to stop in an emergency, react as soon as you can while keeping control of the vehicle. Keep both hands on the steering wheel so you can control the vehicle's direction of travel.

33. Before moving off, you should use both the interior and exterior mirrors to check that the road is clear. Look around to check the blind spots and, if necessary, give a signal to warn other road users of your intentions.

34. Never attempt to use a hand-held phone while you're driving, except in a genuine emergency. It's illegal and will take your attention away from driving, putting you at greater risk of causing a collision.

35. It's easy to lose your way in an unfamiliar area. If you need to check a map or ask for directions, first find a safe place to stop.

36. Windscreen pillars can obstruct your view, particularly at bends and junctions. Look out for other road users – especially cyclists, motorcyclists and pedestrians – as they can easily be hidden by this obstruction.

37. If you want to turn your car around, try to find a place where you have good all-round vision. If this isn't possible, and you're unable to see clearly, then get someone to guide you.

38. Modern vehicles provide the driver with a good view of both the road ahead and behind using well-positioned mirrors. However, the mirrors can't see every angle of the scene behind and to the sides of the vehicle. This is why it's essential that you know when and how to check your blind spots, so that you're aware of any hidden hazards.

39. Talking to someone while you're driving can distract you and, unlike someone in the car with you, the person on the other end of a mobile phone is unable to see the traffic situations you're dealing with. They won't stop speaking to you even if you're approaching a hazardous situation. You need to concentrate on your driving all of the time, but especially so when dealing with a hazard.

40. Before emerging right onto a dual carriageway, make sure that the central reservation is deep enough to protect your vehicle. If it isn't, you should treat the dual carriageway as one road and check that it's clear in both directions before pulling out. Neglecting to do this could place part or all of your vehicle in the path of approaching traffic and cause a collision.

41. Windscreen pillars can completely block your view of pedestrians, motorcyclists and cyclists. You should make a particular effort to look for these road users; don't just rely on a quick glance.

42. Vehicle navigation systems can be useful when driving on unfamiliar routes. However, they can also distract you and cause you to lose control if you look at or adjust them while driving. Pull up in a convenient and safe place before adjusting them.

43. Pelican crossings are signal-controlled crossings operated by pedestrians. Push-button controls change the signals. Pelican crossings have no red-and-amber stage before green; instead, they have a flashing amber light. This means you must give way to pedestrians who are already on the crossing. If the crossing is clear, however, you can continue.

44. If people are waiting to use a pedestrian crossing, slow down and be prepared to stop. Don't wave them across the road, because another driver may not have seen them, may not have seen your signal, and may not be able to stop safely.

45. 'Tailgating' is the term used when a driver or rider follows the vehicle in front too closely. It's dangerous because it restricts their view of the road ahead and leaves no safety margin if the vehicle in front needs to slow down or stop suddenly. Tailgating is often the underlying cause of rear-end collisions or multiple pile-ups.

46. Water will reduce your tyres' grip on the road. The safe separation gap of at least two seconds in dry conditions should be doubled, to at least four seconds, in wet weather.

47. A long lorry with a heavy load will need more time to pass you than a car, especially on an uphill stretch of road. Slow down and allow the lorry to pass.

48. Emergency vehicles use blue flashing lights. If you see or hear one, move out of its way as soon as it's safe and legal to do so.

49. Pull over in a place where the ambulance can pass safely. Check that there are no bollards or obstructions in the road that will prevent it from passing.

50. A green flashing beacon on a vehicle means the driver or passenger is a doctor on an emergency call. Give way to them if it's safe to do so. Be aware that the vehicle may be travelling quickly or may stop in a hurry.

51. These signs apply only to tram drivers, but you should know their meaning so that you're aware of the priorities and are able to anticipate the actions of the driver.

52. The narrow wheels of a bicycle can become stuck in the tram rails, causing the cyclist to stop suddenly, wobble or even lose balance altogether. The tram lines are also slippery, which could cause a cyclist to slide or fall off.

53. Your horn mustn't be used between 11.30 pm and 7 am in a built-up area or when you're stationary, unless a moving vehicle poses a danger. Its function is to alert other road users to your presence.

54. When you're in a one-way street and want to turn right, you should take up a position in the right-hand lane. This will allow other road users, not wishing to turn, to pass on the left. Indicate your intention and take up the correct position in good time.

55. If you wish to turn right into a side road, take up your position in good time. Move to the centre of the road when it's safe to do so. This will allow vehicles to pass you on the left. Early planning will show other traffic what you intend to do.

56. A toucan crossing is designed to allow pedestrians and cyclists to cross at the same time. Look out for cyclists approaching the crossing at speed.

57. Don't enforce the speed limit by blocking another vehicle's progress. This will only lead to the other driver becoming more frustrated. Allow the other vehicle to pass when you can do so safely.

58. You should only flash your headlights to warn others of your presence. Don't use them to greet others, show impatience or give priority to other road users, because they could misunderstand your signal.

59. Be cautious, especially when your view is restricted by hedges, bushes, walls, large vehicles, etc. In the summer months, these junctions can become more difficult to deal with, because growing foliage may further obscure your view.

60. In good conditions, the 'two-second rule' can be used to check the distance between your vehicle and the one in front. This technique works on roads carrying faster traffic. Choose a fixed object, such as a bridge, sign or tree. When the vehicle ahead passes this object, say to yourself 'Only a fool breaks the two-second rule.' If you reach the object before you finish saying this, you're too close.

61. Puffin crossings have infra-red sensors that detect when pedestrians are crossing and hold the red traffic signal until the crossing is clear. The use of a sensor means there's no flashing amber phase as there is with a pelican crossing.

62. If the driver behind is following too closely, there's a danger they'll collide with the back of your vehicle if you stop suddenly. You can reduce this risk by slowing down and increasing the safety margin in front of you. This reduces the chance that you'll have to stop suddenly and allows you to spread your braking over a greater distance. This is an example of defensive driving.

63. Use the full-beam headlights only when you can be sure that you won't dazzle other road users.

64. Large, long vehicles need extra room when making turns at junctions. They may move out to the right in order to make a left turn. Keep well back and don't attempt to pass them on their left.

65. In queuing traffic, your brake lights can dazzle drivers behind you. If you apply your parking brake, you can take your foot off the footbrake. This will deactivate the brake lights.

66. Keep a steady course to give the driver behind an opportunity to overtake safely. If necessary, slow down. Reacting incorrectly to another driver's impatience can lead to danger.

67. Bus-lane signs show the vehicles allowed to use the lane and also its times of operation. Where no times are shown, the bus lane is in operation 24 hours a day.

68. If someone in charge of animals asks you to stop, you should do so and switch off your engine. Animals are unpredictable and startle easily; they could turn and run into your path or into the path of another moving vehicle.

69. Horses can be startled by the sound of a car engine or the rush of air caused by a vehicle passing too closely. Keep well back and only pass when it's safe. Leave them plenty of room; you may have to use the other side of the road to go past safely.

70. As you approach a zebra crossing, look for pedestrians waiting to cross. Where you can see them, slow down and prepare to stop. Be especially careful of children and older people, who may have difficulty judging when it's safe to cross.

71. Try to be ready for the unexpected. Plan ahead and learn to anticipate hazards. You'll then give yourself more time to react to any problems that might occur.

72. A sensor will automatically detect that the pedestrians have reached a safe position. Don't drive on until the green light shows and it's safe for you to do so.

73. In good, dry conditions, a driver needs to keep a distance of at least two seconds from the car in front. This should allow enough space for you to stop if the driver in front has to stop suddenly.

74. If you follow another vehicle with your headlights on full beam, they could dazzle the driver. Leave a safe distance and make sure that the light from your dipped beam falls short of the vehicle in front.

75. If you're driving a slow-moving vehicle along a narrow road, try not to hold up faster traffic. If you see vehicles following behind, pull over in a safe place and let the traffic pass before continuing. Don't wave other traffic past – this could be dangerous if you or they haven't seen any hazard that's hidden from view.

76. Diesel fuel can spill out if your filler cap isn't secured properly. This is most likely to occur on bends, junctions and roundabouts, where it will make the road slippery, especially if it's wet. At the end of a dry spell of weather, the road surfaces may have a high level of diesel spillage that hasn't been washed away by rain.

77. When learning to drive, it's a good idea to practise filling your car with fuel. Ask your instructor if you can use a petrol station and fill the fuel tank yourself. You need to know where the filler cap is on the car you're driving, so you know which side of the pump to park at. Take care not to overfill the tank and make sure you secure the filler cap correctly, so that no fuel leaks onto the road while you're driving.

78. Competitive driving increases the risks to everyone and is the opposite of responsible, considerate and defensive driving. Defensive driving is about questioning the actions of other road users and being prepared for the unexpected. Don't be taken by surprise.

79. Your tyres are your only contact with the road. To prevent problems with braking and steering, keep your tyres free from defects; they must have sufficient tread depth and be correctly inflated. Correct tyre pressures help reduce the risk of skidding and provide a safer and more comfortable drive or ride.

80. Every effort must be made to prevent excessive noise, especially in built-up areas at night. Don't rev your engine or sound the horn unnecessarily. It's illegal to sound your horn in a built-up area between 11.30 pm and 7.00 am, except when another road user poses a danger.

81. Inconsiderate parking can obstruct the flow of traffic and so make traffic congestion worse. Red routes are designed to prevent this by enforcing strict parking restrictions. Driving slowly in traffic increases fuel consumption and causes a build-up of exhaust fumes.

82. Traffic-calming measures help to keep vehicle speeds low in congested areas where there are pedestrians and children. A pedestrian is much more likely to survive a collision with a vehicle travelling at 20 mph than they are with a vehicle travelling at 40 mph.

83. Catalytic converters reduce a large percentage of harmful exhaust emissions. They work more efficiently when the engine has reached its normal working temperature.

84. Check the tyre pressures when the tyres are cold. This will give you a more accurate reading. The heat generated on a long journey will raise the pressure inside the tyre.

85. Check your tyre pressures frequently – normally once a week. If they're lower than those recommended by the manufacturer, there will be more 'rolling resistance'. The engine will have to work harder to overcome this, leading to increased fuel consumption.

86. Batteries contain acid, which is hazardous, and they must be disposed of safely. This means taking them to an appropriate disposal site.

87. Accelerating and braking gently and smoothly will help to save fuel and reduce wear on your vehicle. This makes it better for the environment too.

88. Some modern batteries are maintenance-free. Check your vehicle handbook and, if necessary, make sure that the plates in each battery cell are covered with fluid.

89. When parking at night, park in the direction of the traffic. This will enable other road users to see the reflectors on the rear of your vehicle. Use your parking lights if the speed limit is over 30 mph.

90. Engines that burn fossil fuels produce exhaust emissions that are harmful to health. The harder you make the engine work, the more emissions it will produce. Engines also use more fuel and produce higher levels of emissions when they're cold. Anything you can do to reduce your use of fossil fuels will help the environment.

91. If you see that parts of the tread on your tyres are wearing before others, it may indicate a brake, steering or suspension fault. Regular servicing will help to detect faults at an early stage and this will avoid the risk of minor faults becoming serious or even dangerous.

92. When approaching a junction where the traffic lights have failed, you should proceed with caution. Treat the situation as an unmarked junction and be prepared to stop.

93. Planning your journey before you set out can help to make it much easier and more pleasant, and may help to ease traffic congestion. Look at a map to help you do this. You may need maps of different scales, depending on where and how far you're going. Printing or writing out the route can also help.

94. No-one likes to spend time in traffic queues. Try to avoid busy times related to school or work travel.

95. If possible, avoid the early morning, late afternoon and early evening 'rush hour'. Doing this should allow you to travel in a more relaxed frame of mind, concentrate solely on what you're doing and arrive at your destination feeling less stressed.

96. It can be frustrating and worrying to find your planned route is blocked by roadworks or diversions. If you've planned an alternative, you'll feel less stressed and more able to concentrate fully on your driving or riding. If your original route is mostly on motorways, it's a good idea to plan an alternative using non-motorway roads. Always carry a map with you just in case you need to refer to it.

97. Always allow plenty of time for your journey in case of unforeseen problems. Anything can happen; for example, punctures, breakdowns, road closures, diversions and delays. You'll feel less stressed and less inclined to take risks if you aren't 'pushed for time'.

98. Using the controls smoothly can reduce fuel consumption by about 15%, as well as reducing wear and tear on your vehicle. Plan ahead and anticipate changes of speed well in advance. This will reduce the need to accelerate rapidly or brake sharply.

99. You should carry out frequent checks on all fluid levels but particularly brake fluid. As the brake pads or shoes wear down, the brake fluid level will drop. If it drops below the minimum mark on the fluid reservoir, air could enter the hydraulic system and lead to a loss of braking efficiency or even complete brake failure.

100. Uneven wear on your tyres can be caused by the condition of your vehicle. Having the vehicle serviced regularly will ensure that the brakes, steering, suspension and wheel alignment are maintained in good order.

101. Brakes can overheat and lose efficiency when they're used continually, such as on a long, steep, downhill stretch of road. Using a lower gear when you drive downhill can help prevent the vehicle from gaining speed.

102. Consult the vehicle handbook or a garage before driving the vehicle any further. Only drive to a garage if it's safe to do so. If you aren't sure, get expert help.

103. When you're going to drive, make sure that you're wearing suitable clothing. Comfortable shoes will ensure that you have proper control of the foot pedals.

104. If you're involved in a collision, head restraints will reduce the risk of neck injury. They must be properly adjusted. Make sure they aren't positioned too low: in a crash, this could cause damage to the neck.

105. If you find that your vehicle bounces as you drive around a corner or bend in the road, the shock absorbers might be worn. Press down on the front wing and, if the vehicle continues to bounce, take it to be checked by a qualified mechanic.

106. A roof rack increases your car's wind resistance. This will cause an increase in fuel consumption, so you should remove it when it isn't being used. An aerodynamically designed roof rack or box will help reduce wind resistance to a minimum, but the rack or box should still be removed when it isn't in use.

107. Your tyres may be of different treads and makes. They can even be second-hand, as long as they're in good condition. They must, however, be intact, without cuts or tears. When checking the side walls for cuts and bulges, don't forget to check the side of the tyre that's hidden from view, under the car.

108. Car tyres must have sufficient depth of tread to give them a good grip on the road surface. The legal minimum for cars is 1.6 mm. This depth should be across the central three-quarters of the breadth of the tyre and around the entire circumference.

109. Seat belts save lives and reduce the risk of injury. If you're carrying passengers under 14 years old, it's your responsibility as the driver to ensure that their seat belts are fastened or they're seated in an approved child restraint.

110. Rapid acceleration and heavy braking lead to increased fuel consumption and vehicle wear

111. If you don't have your vehicle serviced regularly, the engine will gradually become less efficient. This will cause increased fuel consumption and, in turn, an increase in the amount of harmful emissions it produces.

112. Try not to use your car as a matter of routine. For shorter journeys, consider walking or cycling instead – this is much better for both you and the environment.

113. Wasting fuel costs you money and also causes unnecessary pollution. Ensuring your tyres are correctly inflated, avoiding carrying unnecessary weight and removing a roof rack that's not in use will all help to reduce your fuel consumption.

114. Unless exempt, you and your passengers must wear a seat belt (or suitable child restraint). The seat belts in your car must be in good condition and working properly; they'll be checked during its MOT test.

115. Your vehicle will use less fuel if you avoid heavy acceleration. The higher the engine revs, the more fuel you'll use. Using the same gear, and covering the same distance, a vehicle travelling at 70 mph will use up to 30% more fuel than it would at 50 mph. However, don't travel so slowly that you inconvenience or endanger other road users.

116. The brakes on your vehicle must be effective and properly adjusted. If your vehicle pulls to one side when braking, take it to be checked by a qualified mechanic as soon as you can.

117. If your wheels are out of balance, it will cause the steering to vibrate at certain speeds. This isn't a fault that will put itself right, so take your vehicle to a garage or tyre fitter to have the wheels rebalanced.

118. Turning the steering wheel when the car isn't moving is known as dry steering. It can cause unnecessary wear to the tyres and steering mechanism.

119. If you have to leave valuables in your car, lock them out of sight. This is the best way to deter an opportunist thief.

120. Having your car registration number etched on all your windows is a cheap and effective way to deter professional car thieves.

121. Never leave the vehicle registration document inside your car. This document would help a thief to dispose of your car more easily.

122. An unlocked car is an open invitation to thieves. Leaving the keys in the ignition not only makes your car easy to steal but could also invalidate your insurance.

123. Harsh braking, frequent gear changes and harsh acceleration increase fuel consumption. An engine uses less fuel when travelling at a constant low speed.

124. It's illegal to pour engine oil down any drain. Oil is a pollutant and harmful to wildlife. Dispose of it safely at an authorised site.

125. Emission tests are carried out to make sure your vehicle's engine is operating efficiently. This ensures the pollution produced by the engine is kept to a minimum. If your vehicle isn't serviced regularly, it may fail the annual MOT test.

126. By looking well ahead and recognising hazards in good time, you can avoid late and heavy braking. Watch the traffic flow and look well ahead for potential hazards so you can control your speed in good time. Avoid over-revving the engine and accelerating harshly, as this increases wear to the engine and uses more fuel.

127. All vehicles need to be serviced to keep working efficiently. An efficient engine uses less fuel and produces fewer harmful emissions than an engine that's running inefficiently. Keeping the vehicle serviced to the manufacturer's schedule should also make it more reliable and reduce the chance of it breaking down.

128. The humps are there for a reason – to protect vulnerable road users by reducing the speed of traffic. Don't accelerate harshly between the humps. Put the safety of others first and maintain a reduced speed throughout the zone.

129. An engine can use more oil during long journeys than on shorter trips. Insufficient engine oil is potentially dangerous: it can lead to excessive wear, mechanical breakdown and expensive repairs.

130. It's an offence to park on the zigzag lines of a zebra crossing. You'll be causing an obstruction by obscuring the view of both pedestrians and drivers.

131. Always switch off the engine, remove the key and lock your car, even if you're only leaving it for a few minutes.

132. Whenever possible, leave your car in a secure car park. This will help deter thieves.

133. Don't park your vehicle where it may obstruct access to a business or property. Think carefully before you slow down and stop. Look at road markings and signs to ensure that you aren't parking illegally.

134. In a collision, rapid deceleration will violently throw vehicle occupants forward and then backwards as the vehicle stops. Seat belts and airbags protect occupants against the forward movement. Head restraints should be adjusted so they give maximum protection to the head and neck during the backward movement.

135. Avoid using your car for short journeys. On a short journey, the engine is unlikely to warm up fully and will therefore be running less efficiently. This will result in the car using more fuel and producing higher levels of harmful emissions.

136. Using a vehicle for short journeys means the engine doesn't have time to reach its normal operating temperature. When an engine is running below its normal operating temperature, it produces increased amounts of pollution. Walking and cycling don't create pollution and have health benefits as well.

137. When leaving your car, take all valuables with you if you can. Otherwise, lock them out of sight.

138. A security-coded radio can deter thieves, as it's likely to be of little use when removed from the vehicle.

139. Having your vehicle broken into or stolen can be very distressing and inconvenient. Avoid leaving your vehicle unattended in poorly-lit areas.

140. The vehicle watch scheme helps to reduce the risk of your car being stolen. By displaying high-visibility vehicle watch stickers in your car, you're inviting the police to stop your vehicle if it's seen in use between midnight and 5 am.

141. Although carbon dioxide is still produced, a catalytic converter fitted to the exhaust system reduces the toxic and polluting gases by up to 90%.

142. By driving smoothly, you'll not only save about 15% of your fuel but will also reduce the amount of wear and tear on your vehicle and the level of pollution it produces. You're also likely to feel more relaxed and have a more pleasant journey.

143. Missing out intermediate gears, when appropriate, helps to reduce the amount of time spent accelerating and decelerating – the times when your vehicle uses the most fuel.

144. Ecosafe driving is all about becoming a more environmentally friendly driver. This will make your journeys more comfortable, as well as considerably reducing your fuel bills and reducing emissions that can damage the environment.

145. The emphasis is on hazard awareness and planning ahead. By looking well ahead, you'll have plenty of time to deal with hazards safely and won't need to brake sharply. This will also reduce damage to the environment.

146. Trailers and caravans may be left in storage over the winter months, and tyres can deteriorate. It's important to check their tread depth and also their pressures and general condition. The legal tread depth of 1.6 mm applies to the central three-quarters of a tyre's breadth, over its entire circumference.

147. Accelerating uses a lot of fuel, so always try to use the accelerator smoothly. Taking your foot off the accelerator allows the momentum of the car to take you forward, especially when going downhill. This can save a considerable amount of fuel without any loss of control over the vehicle.

148. If you have adult passengers, it's their responsibility to wear a seat belt, but you should still remind them to use one as they get in the car. It's your responsibility to make sure that all children in your car are secured with an appropriate restraint. Exemptions are allowed for those with a medical exemption certificate.

149. Passengers should always be secured and safe. Children should be encouraged to fasten their seat belts or approved restraints themselves from an early age, so that it becomes a matter of routine. As the driver, you must check that they're fastened securely. It's your responsibility.

150. Too much oil in the engine will create excess pressure and could damage engine seals and cause oil leaks. Any excess oil should be drained off.

151. Usually, a correct child restraint must be used. In cases where one isn't available, an adult seat belt must be used instead. In a collision, unrestrained objects and people can cause serious injury or even death.

152. As the driver, it's your responsibility to make sure that children are secure and safe in your vehicle. Make yourself familiar with the rules. In a few very exceptional cases when a child restraint isn't available, an adult seat belt must be used.

153. If your vehicle is stationary and is likely to remain so for some time, switch off the engine. We should all try to reduce global warming and pollution.

154. It's illegal to fit a rear-facing baby seat into a passenger seat protected by an active frontal airbag. If the airbag activates, it could cause serious injury or even death to the child. You must secure it in a different seat or deactivate the relevant airbag. Follow the manufacturer's advice when fitting a baby seat.

155. When you leave your vehicle parked on a road, switch off the engine and secure the vehicle. Make sure no valuables are visible, shut all the windows, lock the vehicle, and set the alarm the vehicle has one.

156. Tyre grip is greatly reduced in icy conditions. For this reason, you need to allow up to ten times the stopping distance you would allow on dry roads.

157. Always give cyclists plenty of room when overtaking them. You need to give them even more room when it's windy. A sudden gust could easily blow them off course and into your path.

158. Doing this will give you an earlier view around the bend and enable you to see any hazards sooner. It also reduces the risk of collision with an oncoming vehicle that may have drifted over the centre line while taking the bend.

159. Water on the brakes will act as a lubricant, causing them to work less efficiently. Using the brakes lightly as you go along will quickly dry them out.

160. If the road surface becomes very hot, it can soften. Tyres are unable to grip a soft surface as well as they can a firm dry one. Take care when cornering and braking.

161. In windy conditions, care must be taken on exposed roads. A strong gust of wind can blow you off course. Watch out for other road users who are particularly likely to be affected, such as cyclists, motorcyclists, high-sided lorries and vehicles towing trailers.

162. Note that this is the typical stopping distance. It will take at least this distance to think, brake and stop in good conditions. In poor conditions, it will take much longer.

163. This distance is the equivalent of 18 car lengths. Try pacing out 73 metres and then look back. It's probably further than you think.

164. Wet weather will affect the time it takes for you to stop and can affect your control. Your speed should allow you to stop safely and in good time. If another vehicle pulls into the gap you've left, ease back until you've regained your stopping distance.

165. Even in good conditions, it will usually take you further than you think to stop. Don't just learn the figures; make sure you understand how far the distance is.

166. Stopping distances are affected by a number of variables. These include the type, model and condition of your vehicle, the road and weather conditions, and your reaction time. Look well ahead for hazards and leave enough space between you and the vehicle in front. This should allow you to pull up safely if you have to, without braking sharply.

167. In strong winds, riders of two-wheeled vehicles are particularly vulnerable. When you overtake them, allow plenty of room. Always check to the left as you pass.

168. Be aware that this is just the braking distance. You need to add the thinking distance to this to give the overall stopping distance. At 50 mph, the typical thinking distance will be 15 metres (50 feet), plus a braking distance of 38 metres (125 feet), giving an overall stopping distance of 53 metres (175 feet). The stopping distance could be greater than this, depending on your attention and response to any hazards. These figures are a general guide.

169. On busy roads, traffic may still travel at high speeds despite being close together. Don't follow the vehicle in front too closely. If a driver behind seems to be 'pushing' you, gradually increase your distance from the vehicle in front by slowing down gently. This will give you more space in front if you have to brake, and will reduce the risk of a collision involving several vehicles.

170. When it's foggy, use dipped headlights. This will help you see and be seen by other road users. If visibility is seriously reduced, consider using front and rear fog lights if you have them. Keep to a sensible speed and don't follow the vehicle in front too closely. If the road is wet and slippery, you'll need to allow twice the normal stopping distance.

171. In a contraflow system, you'll be travelling close to oncoming traffic and sometimes in narrow lanes. You should get into the correct lane in good time, obey any temporary speed-limit signs and keep a safe separation distance from the vehicle ahead.

172. If you're travelling on an icy road, extra caution will be required to avoid loss of control. Keeping your speed down and using the highest gear possible will reduce the risk of the tyres losing their grip on this slippery surface.

173. Skidding is usually caused by driver error. You should always adjust your driving to take account of the road and weather conditions.

174. Harsh use of the accelerator, brakes or steering is likely to lead to skidding, especially on slippery surfaces. Avoid steering and braking at the same time. In icy conditions it's very important that you constantly assess what's ahead, so that you can take appropriate action in plenty of time.

175. To correct a skid, you need to steer into it. However, be careful not to overcorrect with too much steering, as this may cause a skid in the opposite direction. Skids don't just happen; they're caused – usually by the driver. Factors increasing the likelihood of a skid include the condition of the vehicle (especially its tyres) and the road and weather conditions.

176. Driving in bad weather increases your risk of having a collision. If you absolutely have to travel, clear your lights, mirrors, number plates and windows of any snow or ice, so that you can see and be seen.

177. If you attempt to move off in a low gear, there will be more torque (turning force) at the driven wheels than if you use a higher gear. More torque makes it easier for the tyres to lose grip and so spin the wheels.

178. In snowy conditions, be careful with the steering, accelerator and brakes. Braking sharply while you're driving on snow is likely to make your car skid.

179. By driving all four wheels, the vehicle has maximum grip on the road. This grip is especially helpful when travelling on slippery or uneven surfaces. However, having four-wheel drive doesn't replace the skills you need to drive safely.

180. When driving down a steep hill, gravity will cause your vehicle to speed up. This will make it more difficult for you to stop. To help keep your vehicle's speed under control, select a lower gear to give you more engine braking and make careful use of the brakes.

181. Turning the wheels towards the kerb will allow them to act as a chock, preventing any forward movement of the vehicle. It will also help to leave your car in gear, or select 'Park' if you have an automatic.

182. Many towns have road humps as part of traffic-calming measures, designed to slow down traffic. Reduce your speed when driving over them. If you go too fast, you could lose control or damage your car. Look out for pedestrians or cyclists while you're driving in these areas.

183. The anti-lock braking system (ABS) will operate when the brakes have been applied harshly and the wheels are about to lock, such as during an emergency. ABS will reduce the likelihood of your car skidding, but it isn't a substitute for safe and responsible driving.

184. Poor contact with the road surface could cause one or more of the tyres to lose grip on the road. This is more likely to happen when braking in poor weather conditions and when the road has a loose, slippery or uneven surface.

185. Anti-lock brakes won't be needed when you're braking normally. Looking well down the road and anticipating possible hazards could prevent you from having to brake late and harshly. Knowing that you have anti-lock brakes isn't an excuse to drive in a careless or reckless way.

186. If the wheels of your vehicle lock, they won't grip the road and you'll lose steering control. In good conditions, the anti-lock braking system (ABS) will prevent the wheels from locking and you'll keep control of your steering. In poor weather conditions or on loose surfaces, the ABS may be less effective.

187. You may have to stop in an emergency due to a misjudgement by another driver or a hazard arising suddenly, such as a child running out into the road. If your vehicle has anti-lock brakes, you should apply the brakes immediately and keep them firmly applied until you stop.

188. Anti-lock brakes may be ineffective on gravel or loose surfaces. They may also be ineffective in very wet weather, when water can build up between the tyre and the road surface; this is known as aquaplaning.

189. Drive extremely carefully when the roads are icy. When travelling on ice, tyres make virtually no noise and the steering feels light and unresponsive.

190. If you drive at speed in very wet conditions, your steering may suddenly feel lighter than usual. This means that the tyres have lifted off the surface of the road and are skating on the surface of the water. This is known as aquaplaning. Reduce speed but don't brake until your steering returns to normal.

191. Extra care should be taken in wet weather. On wet roads, your stopping distance could be double that in dry conditions.

192. One way of checking there's a safe distance between you and the vehicle in front is to use the two-second rule. To check for a two-second time gap, choose a stationary object ahead, such as a bridge or road sign. When the car in front passes the object, say 'Only a fool breaks the two-second rule'. If you reach the object before you finish saying the phrase, you're too close and need to increase the gap.

193. When driving on downhill stretches of road, selecting a lower gear gives increased engine braking. This will prevent excessive use of the brakes, which become less effective if they overheat.

194. If you have ABS and need to stop in an emergency, keep your foot firmly on the brake pedal until the vehicle has stopped. When the ABS operates, you may hear a grating sound and feel vibration through the brake pedal. This is normal and you should maintain pressure on the brake pedal until the vehicle stops.

195. If your car is fitted with anti-lock brakes, they'll only activate when they sense that the wheels are about to lock. By preventing the wheels from locking, you'll be able to steer to avoid the hazard, while maximum braking is also applied.

196. When surface spray reduces visibility, switch on your dipped headlights. This will help other road users to see you.

197. Coasting is the term used when the clutch is held down, or the gear lever is in neutral, and the vehicle is allowed to freewheel. This reduces the driver's control of the vehicle. When you coast, the engine can't drive the wheels to stabilise you through a corner, or give the assistance of engine braking to help slow the car.

198. Don't venture out if your journey isn't necessary. If you have to travel and someone is expecting you at the other end, let them know that you'll be taking longer than usual for your journey. This will stop them worrying if you don't turn up on time and will also take the pressure off you, so you don't feel you have to rush.

199. Be tolerant if a vehicle emerges and you have to brake quickly. Anyone can make a mistake, so don't react aggressively. Be alert where there are side roads and be especially careful where there are parked vehicles, because these can make it difficult for emerging drivers to see you.

200. Be tolerant of older drivers. They may take longer to react to a hazard and they may be hesitant in some situations – for example, at a junction.

201. Try to plan your journey so that you can take rest stops. It's recommended that you take a break of at least 15 minutes after every two hours of driving or riding. This should help to maintain your concentration.

202. When approaching a junction where the traffic lights have failed, you should proceed with caution. Treat the situation as an unmarked junction and be prepared to stop.

203. You should never overtake as you approach a junction. If a vehicle emerged from the junction while you were overtaking, a dangerous situation could develop very quickly.

204. Although a convex mirror gives a wide view of the scene behind, you should be aware that it won't show you everything behind or to the side of your vehicle. Before you move off, you'll need to look over your shoulder to check for anything not visible in the mirrors.

205. Be cautious and don't attempt to overtake. The driver may be unsure of the location of a junction and may turn suddenly.

206. Traffic-calming measures such as road humps, chicanes and narrowings are intended to slow drivers down to protect vulnerable road users. Don't speed up until you reach the end of the traffic-calmed zone.

207. The names of towns and cities may be painted on the road at busy junctions and complex road systems. Their purpose is to let you move into the correct lane in good time, allowing traffic to flow more freely.

208. If you intend to overtake, you must consider that approaching traffic could be planning the same manoeuvre. When you've considered the situation and decided it's safe, indicate your intentions early. This will show the approaching traffic that you intend to pull out.

209. An amber flashing light on a vehicle indicates that it's slow-moving. Battery-powered vehicles used by disabled people are limited to 8 mph. It isn't advisable for them to be used on dual carriageways where the speed limit exceeds 50 mph. If they are, then an amber flashing light must be used.

210. You should overtake only when it's really necessary and you can see it's clear ahead. Look out for road signs and markings that show it's illegal or would be unsafe to overtake; for example, approaching junctions or bends. In many cases, overtaking is unlikely to significantly improve your journey time.

211. Alcohol will severely reduce your ability to drive or ride safely and there are serious consequences if you're caught over the drink-drive limit. It's known that alcohol can affect your judgement.

212. The continuous white line shows the edge of the carriageway. It can be especially useful when visibility is restricted, such as at night or in bad weather. It's discontinued in some places; for example, at junctions, lay-bys, entrances or other openings.

213. You should always try to keep junctions clear. If you're in queuing traffic, make sure that when you stop you leave enough space for traffic to flow into and out of the junction.

214. Never stop on the hard shoulder to rest. If there's no service area for several miles, leave the motorway at the next exit and find somewhere safe and legal to pull over.

215. When you're turning into a side road, pedestrians who are crossing have priority. You should wait to allow them to finish crossing safely. Be patient if they're slow or unsteady. Don't try to rush them by sounding your horn, flashing your lights, revving your engine or giving any other inappropriate signal.

216. Make sure that you've reduced your speed and are in the correct gear for the turn. Look into the road before you turn and always give way to any pedestrians who are crossing.

217. Never attempt to change direction to the right without first checking your right-hand mirror and blind spot. A motorcyclist might not have seen your signal and could be hidden by other traffic. This observation should become a matter of routine.

218. Toucan crossings are shared by pedestrians and cyclists, who are permitted to cycle across. They're shown the green light together. The signals are push-button-operated and there's no flashing amber phase.

219. If a school crossing patrol steps out into the road with a 'stop' sign, you must stop. Don't wave anyone across the road and don't get impatient or rev your engine.

220. When someone is deaf as well as blind, they may carry a white stick with a red reflective band. They may not be aware that you're approaching and they may not be able to hear anything; so, for example, your horn would be ineffective as a warning to them.

221. Be aware that older people might take a long time to cross the road. They might also be hard of hearing and not hear you approaching. Don't hurry older people across the road by getting too close to them or revving your engine.

222. Older people may have impaired hearing, vision, concentration and judgement. They may also walk slowly and so could take a long time to cross the road.

223. If you're following a cyclist who's signalling to turn right at a roundabout, leave plenty of room. Give them space and time to get into the correct lane.

224. Don't pass cyclists too closely, as they may need to veer around potholes

225. Cyclists and motorcyclists are smaller than other vehicles and so are more difficult to see. They can easily be hidden from your view by cars parked near a junction.

226. If you're waiting to emerge from a side road, look carefully for motorcycles: they can be difficult to see. Be especially careful if there are parked vehicles or other obstructions restricting your view.

227. A motorcycle can be lost from sight behind another vehicle. The use of the headlights helps to make it more conspicuous and therefore more easily seen.

228. Motorcycles and scooters are generally smaller than other vehicles and can be difficult to see. Wearing bright clothing makes it easier for other road users to see a motorcyclist approaching, especially at junctions.

229. When a motorcyclist is travelling slowly, it's likely that they're looking for a turning or entrance. Be patient and stay behind them in case they stop or change direction suddenly.

230. When you see a motorcyclist take a glance over their shoulder, they're probably about to change direction. Recognising a clue like this helps you to anticipate their next action. This can improve road safety for you and others.

231. Pedestrians and riders on two wheels can be harder to see than other road users. Make sure you look for them, especially at junctions. Effective observation, coupled with appropriate action, can save lives.

232. Horse riders often keep to the outside of the roundabout even if they're turning right. Give them plenty of room and remember that they may have to cross lanes of traffic.

233. If the lights turn to green, wait for any pedestrians to clear the crossing. Allow them to finish crossing the road in their own time, and don't try to hurry them by revving your engine.

234. The flashing amber lights are switched on to warn you that children may be crossing near a school. Slow down and take extra care, as you may have to stop.

235. Cyclists approaching a roundabout in the left-hand lane may be turning right but may not have been able to get into the correct lane due to heavy traffic. They may also feel safer keeping to the left all the way around the roundabout. Be aware of them and give them plenty of room.

236. Passing the moped and turning into the junction could mean that you cut across the front of the rider. This might force them to slow down, stop or even lose control. Stay behind the moped until it has passed the junction and then you can turn without affecting the rider.

237. Allow the horse rider to enter and exit the roundabout in their own time. They may feel safer keeping to the left all the way around the roundabout. Don't get up close behind or alongside them, because that would probably upset the horse and create a dangerous situation.

238. Learners might not have confidence when they first start to drive. Allow them plenty of room and don't react adversely to their hesitation. We all learn from experience, but new drivers will have had less practice in dealing with all the situations that might occur.

239. Learning to drive is a process of practice and experience. Try to understand this and tolerate those who make mistakes while they're learning.

240. On a quiet country road, always be aware that there may be a hazard just around the next bend, such as a slow-moving vehicle or pedestrians. Pedestrians are advised to walk on the right-hand side of the road if there's no pavement, so they may be walking towards you on your side of the road.

241. You must show consideration to other road users. The reactions of older drivers may be slower and they might need more time to deal with a situation. Be tolerant and don't lose patience or show annoyance.

242. Make allowances for cyclists, and give them plenty of room. Don't overtake and then immediately turn left. Be patient and turn behind them when they've passed the junction.

243. Horses and their riders move more slowly than other road users. They might not have time to cut across heavy traffic to take up a position in the right-hand lane. For this reason, a horse and rider may approach a roundabout in the left-hand lane even though they're turning right.

244. Powered vehicles used by disabled people are small, low, hard to see and travel very slowly. On a dual carriageway, a flashing amber light will warn other road users.

245. If you want to turn left and there's a cyclist in front of you, hold back. Wait until the cyclist has passed the junction and then turn left behind them. Don't try to intimidate them by driving too closely.

246. Different coloured beacons warn of different types of vehicle needing special attention. Blue beacons are used on emergency vehicles that need priority. Green beacons are found on doctors' cars. Amber beacons generally denote slower moving vehicles, which are often large. These vehicles are usually involved in road maintenance or local amenities and make frequent stops.

247. Be particularly careful when approaching horse riders – slow down and be prepared to stop. Always pass wide and slowly, and look out for signals given by the riders. Horses are unpredictable: always treat them as potential hazards and take great care when passing them.

248. Where street repairs have closed off pavements, proceed carefully and slowly, as pedestrians might have to walk in the road.

249. To avoid being unbalanced, a motorcyclist might swerve to avoid potholes and bumps in the road. Be prepared for this and allow them extra space.

250. Dogs trained to help deaf people have a yellow or burgundy coat. If you see one, you should take extra care, as the pedestrian may not be aware of vehicles approaching.

251. There are some crossings where cycle routes lead cyclists to cross at the same place as pedestrians. These are called toucan crossings. Always look out for cyclists, as they're likely to be approaching faster than pedestrians.

252. These are known as advanced stop lines. When the lights are red (or about to become red), you should stop at the first white line. However, if you've crossed that line as the lights change, you must stop at the second line even if it means you're in the area reserved for cyclists.

253. Before overtaking, assess the situation. Look well ahead to see whether the cyclist will need to change direction. Be especially aware of a cyclist approaching parked vehicles, as they'll need to alter course. Don't pass too closely or cut in sharply.

254. Slow down and be ready to stop if you see animals in the road ahead. Animals are easily frightened by noise and vehicles passing too close to them. Stop if signalled to do so by the person in charge.

255. The people on the walk should be keeping to the left, but don't assume this. Pass carefully, making sure you have time to do so safely. Be aware that the pedestrians have their backs to you and may not know that you're there.

256. New drivers and riders are often involved in a collision or incident early in their driving career. Due to a lack of experience, they may not react to hazards appropriately. Approved training courses are offered by driver and rider training schools for people who have passed their test but want extra training.

257. If you can't tell whether there's anything behind you, it's always safest to check before reversing. There may be a small child or a low obstruction close behind your car.

258. If you need to reverse into a side road, try to find a place that's free from traffic and pedestrians. Look all around before and during the manoeuvre. Stop and give way to any pedestrians who want to cross behind you. Avoid waving them across, sounding the horn, flashing your lights or giving any signals that could mislead them and create a dangerous situation.

259. It may not be possible to see a small child through the rear windscreen of your vehicle. Be aware of this before you reverse. If there are children about, get out and check that it's clear before reversing.

260. If you want to turn right from a junction and your view is restricted, stop. Ease forward until you can see – something might be approaching.

261. A motorcyclist could be riding along the outside of the queue. Always check your mirror before turning, as situations behind you can change in the time you've been waiting to turn.

262. The flashing amber light allows pedestrians already on the crossing to get to the other side before a green light shows to the traffic. Be aware that some pedestrians, such as elderly people and young children, need longer to cross. Let them do this at their own pace.

263. At a pelican crossing, the green light means you may proceed as long as the crossing is clear. If someone hasn't finished crossing, be patient and wait for them, whether they're disabled or not.

264. Beware of children playing in the street and running out into the road. If a ball bounces out from the pavement, slow down and be prepared to stop. Don't encourage anyone to retrieve it. Other road users may not see your signal and you might lead a child into a dangerous situation.

265. In some circumstances, your indicators may be difficult to see and another road user may not realise you're about to turn. A final check in your mirror and blind spot can help you to see an overtaking vehicle, so that you can avoid turning across their path.

266. In queuing traffic, motorcyclists could be passing you on either side. Use your mirrors and check your blind area before changing lanes or changing direction.

267. If you see a bus ahead, watch out for pedestrians. They might not be able to see you if they're crossing from behind the bus.

268. When you decide to overtake a horse rider, make sure you can do so safely before you move out. Leave them plenty of room and pass slowly. Passing too closely at speed could startle the horse and unseat the rider.

269. If you're driving in high winds, be aware that the conditions might force a motorcyclist or cyclist to swerve or wobble. Take this into consideration if you're following or wish to overtake a two-wheeled vehicle.

270. Motorcyclists and cyclists are often more difficult to see at junctions. They're easily hidden from view and you may not be able to see them approaching a junction if your view is partially blocked; for example, by other traffic.

271. Scan the road as you drive. Try to anticipate hazards by being aware of the places where they're likely to occur. You'll then be able to react in good time.

272. The interior mirror of most vehicles can be set to an anti-dazzle position. You'll still be able to see the lights of the traffic behind you, but the dazzle will be greatly reduced.

273. You should slow down and be prepared to stop, as you would for an able-bodied person. Don't wave them across, as other traffic may not stop.

274. Large vehicles can hide other vehicles that are overtaking – especially motorcycles, which may be filtering past queuing traffic. You need to be aware of the possibility of hidden vehicles and not assume that it's safe to emerge.

275. When following a large vehicle, keep well back. If you're too close, you won't be able to see the road ahead and the driver of the long vehicle might not be able to see you in their mirrors.

276. There might be pedestrians crossing from in front of the bus. Look out for them if you intend to pass. Consider how many people are waiting to get on the bus - check the queue if you can. The bus might move off straight away if no-one is waiting to get on.

277. Large vehicles throw up a lot of spray when it's wet. This makes it difficult for following drivers to see the road ahead. You'll be able to see more by dropping back further, out of the spray. This will also increase your separation distance, giving you more room to stop if you have to.

278. Sometimes your separation distance is shortened by a driver moving into the gap you've allowed. When this happens, react positively, stay calm and drop further back to re-establish a safe following distance.

279. When you're following a long vehicle, stay well back so that you can get a better view of the road ahead. The closer you get, the less you'll be able to see of the road. Be patient and don't take a gamble. Only overtake when you're certain that you can complete the manoeuvre safely.

280. Although cars are the least likely to be affected, side winds can take anyone by surprise. This is most likely to happen after overtaking a large vehicle, when passing gaps between hedges or buildings, and on exposed sections of road.

281. Some powered wheelchairs and mobility scooters are designed for use on the pavement only and cannot exceed 4 mph (6 km/h). Others can go on the road as well, and this category cannot exceed 8 mph (12 km/h). Take great care around these vehicles. They're extremely vulnerable because of their low speed and small size.

282. Depending on relative speed, it will usually take you longer to pass a lorry than other vehicles. Hazards to watch for include oncoming traffic, junctions ahead, bends or dips that could restrict

your view, and signs or road markings that prohibit overtaking. Make sure you can see that it's safe to complete the manoeuvre before you start to overtake.

283. Windy weather affects motorcyclists more than other vehicles. In windy conditions, high-sided vehicles cause air turbulence. You should keep well back, as the motorcyclist could be blown off course.

284. As you approach, look out for any signal the driver might make. If you pass the vehicle, watch out for pedestrians attempting to cross the road from behind the bus. They'll be hidden from view until the last moment.

285. You should take extra care when you first encounter trams. You'll have to get used to dealing with a different traffic system.

286. Towing a large trailer or caravan can greatly reduce your view of the road behind. You may need to fit extended-arm side mirrors so that you can see clearly behind and down both sides of the caravan or trailer.

287. You must make sure that other road users can see you, but you don't want to dazzle them. Use your dipped headlights during the day if visibility is poor. If visibility falls below 100 metres (328 feet), you may use your rear fog lights, but don't forget to turn them off when the visibility improves.

288. Cyclists, and motorcyclists, are very vulnerable in high winds. They can easily be blown well off course and veer into your path. Always allow plenty of room when overtaking them. Passing too close could cause a draught and unbalance the rider.

289. You may pass slower vehicles on their left while travelling along a one-way street. Be aware of drivers who may need to change lanes and may not expect faster traffic passing on their left.

290. The road will be very wet and spray from other vehicles will reduce your visibility. Tyre grip will also be reduced, increasing your stopping distance. You should at least double your separation distance.

291. Don't overtake if there's a possibility of a road junction, bend or brow of a bridge or hill ahead. There are many hazards that are difficult to see in the dark. Only overtake if you're certain that the road ahead is clear. Don't take a chance.

292. The purpose of a box junction is to keep the junction clear by preventing vehicles from stopping in the path of crossing traffic.

293. Traffic-calming measures make the roads safer for vulnerable road users, such as cyclists, pedestrians and children. These can be designed as chicanes, road humps or other obstacles that encourage drivers and riders to slow down.

294. Be especially careful if you're on a motorway in fog. Reflective studs are there to help you in poor visibility. Different colours are used so that you'll know which lane you're in.

295. A rumble device consists of raised markings or strips across the road, designed to give drivers an audible, visual and tactile warning. These devices are used in various locations, including in the line separating the hard shoulder and the left-hand lane on the motorway and on the approach to some hazards, to alert drivers to the need to slow down.

296. If you're planning to make a journey when it's foggy, listen to the weather reports. If visibility is very poor, avoid making unnecessary journeys. If you do travel, leave plenty of time – and if someone is waiting for you to arrive, let them know that your journey will take longer than normal. This will also take off any pressure you may feel to rush.

297. To prevent your lights from dazzling the driver of the car in front, wait until you've passed them before switching to full beam.

298. Be patient and stay behind the car in front. You shouldn't normally overtake other vehicles in areas subject to traffic calming. If you overtake here, you may easily exceed the speed limit, defeating the purpose of the traffic-calming measures.

299. Trams may run on roads used by other vehicles and pedestrians. The section of road used by trams is known as the reserved area and should be kept clear. It usually has a different surface, edged with white lane markings.

300. Take care when using single-track roads. It can be difficult to see around bends, because of hedges or fences, so expect to meet oncoming vehicles. Drive carefully and be ready to pull into or stop opposite a passing place, where you can pass each other safely.

301. Other drivers or riders may have to change course due to the size or characteristics of their vehicle. Understanding this will help you to anticipate their actions. Motorcyclists and cyclists will be checking the road ahead for uneven or slippery surfaces, especially in wet weather. They may need to move across their lane to avoid surface hazards such as potholes and drain covers.

302. You won't be able to see as far ahead in fog as you can on a clear day. You'll need to reduce your speed so that, if a hazard looms out of the fog, you have the time and space to take avoiding action.

303. The engine will need more power to pull the vehicle up the hill. When approaching a steep hill you should select a lower gear to help maintain your speed. You should do this without hesitation, so that you don't lose too much speed before engaging the lower gear.

304. The draught caused by other vehicles – particularly those with high sides – could be strong enough to push you out of your lane. Be prepared for a sudden gust of wind as you pass large vehicles. Keep both hands on the steering wheel to help you keep full control.

305. If your car skids and the rear wheels slide to the right, you need to steer into the skid (ie to the right), until the front and rear wheels are brought into line. Don't oversteer or you'll cause a skid in the opposite direction and this will make the situation worse.

306. If you're following another road user in fog, stay well back. The driver in front won't be able to see hazards until they're close and might need to brake suddenly. Also, the road surface is likely to be wet and could be slippery.

307. If you have to park your vehicle in foggy conditions, try to find a place to park off the road. If this isn't possible, park on the road facing in the same direction as the traffic. Leave your sidelights switched on and make sure they're clean.

308. If the headlights of an oncoming vehicle dazzle you, slow down or, if necessary, stop. Don't close your eyes or swerve, as you'll increase your chances of having a collision. Don't flash your headlights either, as this could dazzle other drivers and make the situation worse.

309. Your fog lights must only be used when visibility is reduced to 100 metres (328 feet) or less. You need to be familiar with the layout of your dashboard so you're aware if your fog lights have been switched on in error, or you've forgotten to switch them off.

310. Switch off your fog lights if the weather improves, but be prepared to use them again if visibility reduces to less than 100 metres (328 feet).

311. Don't forget to switch off your fog lights when the weather improves. You could be prosecuted for driving with them on in good visibility. The high intensity of rear fog lights can dazzle following drivers and make your brake lights difficult to notice.

312. Rear fog lights shine more brightly than normal rear lights, so that they show up in reduced visibility. When the visibility improves, you must switch them off; this stops them dazzling the driver behind.

313. Chains can be fitted to your wheels in snowy conditions. They can help you to move off without wheelspin, or to keep moving in deep snow. You'll still need to adjust your driving to suit these conditions.

314. You should brake and slow down before selecting a lower gear. The gear can then be used to keep the speed low and help you control the vehicle. This is particularly helpful on long downhill stretches, where brake fade can occur if the brakes overheat.

315. Letting your vehicle roll or coast in neutral reduces your control over steering and braking. This can be dangerous on downhill slopes, where your vehicle could pick up speed very quickly.

316. Don't travel in icy or snowy weather unless your journey is essential.

317. If you're driving on a motorway at night or in poor visibility, you must always use your headlights, even if the road is well lit. Other road users must be able to see you, but you should avoid causing dazzle.

318. If you're driving behind other traffic on the motorway at night, use dipped headlights. Main-beam headlights will dazzle the other drivers. Your headlights' dipped beam should fall short of the vehicle in front.

319. Having tyres correctly inflated and in good condition will ensure they have maximum grip on the road; how well your tyres grip the road has a significant effect on your car's stopping distance.

320. Always use your headlights at night on a motorway unless you've had to stop on the hard shoulder. If you break down and have to use the hard shoulder, switch off your headlights but leave your sidelights on, so that other road users can see your vehicle.

321. When you take your foot off the accelerator, engines have a natural resistance to turn, caused mainly by the cylinder compression. Changing to a lower gear requires the engine to turn faster and so it will have greater resistance than when it's made to turn more slowly. When going downhill, changing to a lower gear will therefore help to keep the vehicle's speed in check.

322. Only use your fog lights when visibility is seriously reduced. Use dipped headlights in poor conditions because this helps other road users to see you without the risk of causing dazzle.

323. Rear fog lights make it easier to spot a vehicle ahead in foggy conditions. Avoid the temptation to use other vehicles' lights as a guide, as they may give you a false sense of security.

324. It's illegal to use your fog lights in conditions other than when visibility is seriously reduced; that is, less than 100 metres (328 feet). Fog lights are very bright and, if you use them when visibility has improved, you could dazzle other drivers.

325. Consider whether the increased risk is worth it. If the weather conditions are bad and your journey isn't essential, then don't drive.

326. This is more likely to happen on vehicles fitted with drum brakes, but it can apply to disc brakes as well. Using a lower gear will assist the braking and help you to keep control of your vehicle.

327. If you have to drive in fog, switch your dipped-beam headlights on and keep your windscreen clear. You should always be able to pull up within the distance you can see ahead.

328. You must turn off your fog lights if visibility is more than 100 metres (328 feet). Be prepared for the fact that the fog may be patchy and you may need to turn them on again if the fog returns.

329. If your rear fog lights are left on when it isn't foggy, the glare they cause makes it difficult for road users behind to know whether you're braking or you've just forgotten to turn off your rear fog lights. This can be a particular problem on wet roads and on motorways. If you leave your rear fog lights on at night, road users behind you are likely to be dazzled and this could put them at risk.

330. Holding the clutch down or staying in neutral for too long will cause your vehicle to freewheel. This is known as 'coasting' and it's dangerous because it reduces your control of the vehicle.

331. Driving in neutral or with the clutch down for long periods is known as 'coasting'. There will be no engine braking and your vehicle will pick up speed on downhill slopes. Coasting can be very dangerous because it reduces steering and braking control.

332. Coasting is when you allow the vehicle to freewheel in neutral or with the clutch pedal depressed. Speed will increase as you lose the benefits of engine braking and have less control. You shouldn't coast, especially when approaching hazards such as junctions or bends and when travelling downhill.

333. Try to look ahead and read the road. Plan your approach to junctions and select the correct gear in good time. This will give you the control you need to deal with any hazards that occur..

334. You must use dipped headlights when daytime visibility is seriously reduced, generally to 100 metres (328 feet) or less. You may also use front or rear fog lights, but they must be switched off when visibility improves.

335. If the skid has been caused by braking too hard for the conditions, release the brake. You may then need to reapply and release the brake again. You may need to do this a number of times. This will allow the wheels to turn and so some steering should also be possible.

336. You should give way to traffic already on the motorway. Where possible, traffic may move over to let you in, but don't force your way into the traffic stream. Traffic could be travelling at high speed, so try to match your speed to filter in without affecting the traffic flow.

337. Travelling at the national speed limit doesn't allow you to hog the right-hand lane. Always use the left-hand lane whenever possible. When leaving a motorway, get into the left-hand lane well before your exit. Reduce your speed on the slip road and look out for sharp bends or curves and traffic queuing at roundabouts.

338. On a motorway, all traffic should use the left-hand lane unless overtaking. When overtaking a number of slower vehicles, move back to the left-hand lane when you're safely past. Check your mirrors frequently and don't stay in the middle or right-hand lane if the left-hand lane is free.

339. A vehicle with a trailer is restricted to 60 mph. For this reason, it isn't allowed in the right-hand lane, as it might hold up faster-moving traffic that wishes to overtake in that lane.

340. On a motorway, it's best to use a roadside emergency telephone so that the emergency services are able to find you easily. The location of the nearest telephone is shown by an arrow on marker posts at the edge of the hard shoulder. If you use a mobile, the operator will need to know your exact location. Before you call, find out the number on the nearest marker post. This number will identify your exact location.

341. Signal your intention and build up sufficient speed on the hard shoulder so that you can filter into a safe gap in the traffic. Don't push your way in, causing other traffic to alter speed or direction.

342. Large, slow-moving vehicles can hinder the progress of other traffic. On a steep gradient, an extra crawler lane may be provided for slow-moving vehicles to allow faster-moving traffic to flow more easily.

343. On motorways, reflective studs of various colours are fixed in the road between the lanes. These help you to identify which lane you're in when it's dark or in poor visibility. Amber-coloured studs are found on the right-hand edge of the main carriageway, next to the central reservation.

344. White studs are found between the lanes on motorways. They reflect back the light from your headlights. This is especially useful in bad weather, when visibility is restricted.

345. The studs between the carriageway and the hard shoulder are normally red. These change to green where there's a slip road, helping you to identify slip roads when visibility is poor or when it's dark.

346. Along the hard shoulder there are marker posts at 100-metre intervals. These will direct you to the nearest emergency telephone.

347. Try to join the motorway without affecting the progress of the traffic already travelling on it. Always give way to traffic already on the motorway. At busy times you may have to slow down to merge into slow-moving traffic.

348. Traffic is passing you at speed. If the draught from a large lorry catches you by surprise, it could blow you off balance and even onto the carriageway. By facing the oncoming traffic, you can see approaching lorries and so be prepared for their draught. You'll also be in a position to see other hazards approaching.

349. Red studs are placed between the edge of the carriageway and the hard shoulder. Where slip roads leave or join the motorway, the studs are green.

350. On a three-lane motorway, you should travel in the left-hand lane unless you're overtaking. This applies regardless of the speed at which you're travelling.

351. At roadworks, and especially where a contraflow system is operating, a speed restriction is likely to be in place. Keep to the lower speed limit and don't switch lanes or get too close to the vehicle in front of you.

352. The colours of the reflective studs on the motorway and their locations are red (between hard shoulder and carriageway), white (between lanes), amber (between the carriageway and central reservation), green (along slip road exits and entrances) and yellow (at roadworks and contraflow systems)

353. Collisions often happen at roadworks. Be aware of the speed limits, slow down in good time and keep your distance from the vehicle in front.

354. Motorways mustn't be used by pedestrians, cyclists, motorcycles under 50 cc, certain slow-moving vehicles without permission, and powered wheelchairs/mobility scooters.

355. Traffic on motorways usually travels faster than on other roads. You need to be looking further ahead to give yourself more time to react to any hazard that may develop.

356. Stay in the left-hand lane long enough to get used to the higher speeds of motorway traffic before considering overtaking.

357. You should keep to the left and only use the right-hand lane if you're passing slower-moving traffic.

358. Don't use the hard shoulder for stopping unless it's an emergency. If you want to stop for any other reason, go to the next exit or service station.

359. You must stop if overhead gantry signs show flashing red lights above every lane on the motorway. If any of the other lanes doesn't show flashing red lights or a red cross, you may move into that lane and continue if it's safe to do so.

360. Plan well ahead when approaching a slip road. If you see traffic joining the motorway, move to another lane if it's safe to do so. This can help the flow of traffic joining the motorway, especially at peak times.

361. You should normally travel in the left-hand lane unless you're overtaking a slower-moving vehicle. When you've finished overtaking, move back into the left-hand lane, but don't cut across in front of the vehicle that you've overtaken.

362. Never overtake on the left, unless the traffic is moving in queues and the queue on your right is moving more slowly than the one you're in.

363. Emergency refuge areas are built at the side of the hard shoulder. If you break down, try to get your vehicle into the refuge, where there's an emergency telephone. The phone connects directly to a control centre. Remember to take care when rejoining the motorway, especially if the hard shoulder is being used as a running lane.

364. Traffic officers don't have enforcement powers but are able to stop and direct people on motorways and some 'A' class roads. They only operate in England and work in partnership with the police at incidents, providing a highly trained and visible service. They're recognised by an orange-and-yellow jacket and their vehicle has yellow-and-black markings.

365. Active traffic management operates on some motorways. Within these areas, at certain times, the hard shoulder will be used as a running lane. A red cross above the hard shoulder shows that this lane should only be used for emergencies and breakdowns.

366. A mandatory speed-limit sign above the hard shoulder shows that this part of the road can be used as a running lane between junctions. You must stay within the speed limit. Look out for vehicles that may have broken down and could be blocking the hard shoulder.

367. Smart motorway schemes are intended to reduce congestion and make journey times more reliable. In these areas, the hard shoulder may be used as a running lane to ease congestion at peak times or in the event of an incident. Variable speed limits are used to help keep the traffic moving and to avoid bunching.

368. When a smart motorway is operating, you must follow the mandatory signs on the gantries above each lane, including the hard shoulder. Variable speed limits help keep the traffic moving and also help to prevent bunching.

369. When traffic travels at a constant speed over a longer distance, journey times normally improve. You may feel that you could travel faster for short periods, but this generally leads to bunching and increased overall journey time.

370. Normally, you should only use the hard shoulder for emergencies and breakdowns, and at roadworks when signs direct you to do so. Smart motorways use active traffic management to ease congestion. In these areas, the hard shoulder may be used as a running lane when speed-limit signs are shown directly above.

371. Congestion can be reduced by keeping traffic at a constant speed. At busy times, maximum speed limits are displayed on overhead gantries. These can be varied quickly, depending on the amount of traffic. By keeping to a constant speed on busy sections of motorway, overall journey times are normally improved.

372. You shouldn't normally stop on a motorway, but there may be occasions when you need to do so. If you're unfortunate enough to break down, make every effort to pull up on the hard shoulder.

373. The national speed limit for a car or motorcycle on a motorway is 70 mph. Lower speed limits may be in force; for example, at roadworks. Variable speed limits also operate in some areas when the motorway is very busy. Cars or motorcycles towing trailers are subject to a lower speed limit.

374. Red flashing lights above all lanes mean you must stop and wait. You'll also see a red cross lit up. Don't change lanes, don't continue and don't pull onto the hard shoulder (unless in an emergency).

375. A red cross above the hard shoulder shows that it's closed as a running lane and should only be used for emergencies or breakdowns. On a smart motorway, the hard shoulder may be used as a running lane at busy times. This will be shown by a mandatory speed limit on the gantry above the hard shoulder.

376. If you feel tired, stop at the nearest service area. If that's too far away, leave the motorway at the next exit and find a safe place to stop. You mustn't stop on the carriageway or hard shoulder of a motorway except in an emergency, when in a traffic queue, or when signalled to do so by a police officer, a traffic officer or traffic signals. Plan your journey so that you have regular rest stops.

377. Don't forget that you're towing a trailer. If you're towing a small, light trailer, it won't reduce your vehicle's performance by very much. However, strong winds or buffeting from large vehicles might cause the trailer to snake from side to side. Be aware of your speed and don't exceed the reduced speed limit imposed on vehicles towing trailers.

378. You should drive in the left-hand lane whenever possible. Only use the other lanes for overtaking or when directed to do so by signals. Using other lanes when the left-hand lane is empty can frustrate drivers behind you.

379. Using your hazard warning lights, as well as your brake lights, will give following traffic an extra warning of the problem ahead. Only use them for long enough for your warning to be seen.

380. Park as far to the left as you can and leave the vehicle by the nearside door. Don't attempt even simple repairs. Instead, walk to an emergency telephone on your side of the road and phone for help. While waiting for help to arrive, stay by your car, keeping well away from the carriageway and hard shoulder.

381. It's illegal to reverse, cross the central reservation or drive against the traffic flow on a motorway. If you miss your exit, carry on until you reach the next one. Ask yourself why you missed your exit – if you think that your concentration is fading, take a break before completing your journey.

382. If you can't get your vehicle onto the hard shoulder, use your hazard warning lights to warn others. Leave your vehicle only when you can safely get clear of the carriageway. Don't try to repair the vehicle or attempt to place any warning device on the carriageway.

383. Before you start your journey, make sure that your vehicle can cope with the demands of high-speed driving. You should check a number of things, the main ones being oil, water and tyres. You also need to plan rest stops if you're making a long journey.

384. If the vehicle in front shows its hazard warning lights, there may be an incident, stopped traffic or queuing traffic ahead. By keeping a safe distance from the vehicle in front, you're able to look beyond it and see any hazards well ahead.

385. You'll see the first advance direction sign one mile from a motorway exit. If you're travelling at 60 mph in the right-hand lane, you'll only have about 50 seconds before you reach the countdown markers. There'll be another sign at the half-mile point. Move to the left-hand lane in good time. Don't cut across traffic at the last moment and don't risk missing your exit.

386. You won't be able to drive unaccompanied until you've passed your practical driving test. When you've passed, it's a good idea to ask your instructor to take you for a lesson on the motorway. Alternatively, you could take part in the Pass Plus scheme. This has been created for new drivers and includes motorway driving. Ask your instructor for details.

387. You should use an emergency telephone when you break down on the motorway; only use your mobile if this isn't possible. The emergency services need to know your exact location so they can reach you as quickly as possible. Look for a number on the nearest marker post beside the hard shoulder. Give this number when you call the emergency services.

388. If you're towing a caravan or trailer, you mustn't use the right-hand lane of a motorway with three or more lanes except in certain specified circumstances, such as when lanes are closed.

389. When approaching a contraflow system, reduce speed in good time and obey all speed limits. You may be travelling in a narrower lane than normal, with no permanent barrier between you and the oncoming traffic. Be aware that the hard shoulder may be used for traffic and the road ahead could be obstructed by slow-moving or broken-down vehicles.

390. You should only stop on the hard shoulder in a genuine emergency. Don't stop there to have a rest or picnic, pick up hitchhikers, answer a mobile phone or check a map. If you miss your intended exit, carry on to the next. Never reverse along the hard shoulder.

391. Make sure that you know the speed limit for the road that you're on. The speed limit on a dual carriageway or motorway is 70 mph for cars and motorcycles, unless signs indicate otherwise. The speed limits for different types of vehicle are listed in The Highway Code.

392. There's a 30 mph speed limit where there are street lights unless signs show another limit.

393. The presence of street lights generally indicates that there's a 30 mph speed limit, unless signs tell you otherwise.

394. Following a tractor can be frustrating, but never overtake if you're unsure whether it's safe. Ask yourself: 'Can I see far enough down the road to ensure that I can complete the manoeuvre safely?' It's better to be delayed for a minute or two than to take a chance that may cause a collision.

395. Long vehicles might have to take a slightly different position when approaching the roundabout or going around it. This is to stop the rear of the vehicle cutting in and mounting the kerb.

396. Clearways are in place so that traffic can flow without the obstruction of parked vehicles. Just one parked vehicle can cause an obstruction for all other traffic. You mustn't stop where a clearway is in force, not even to pick up or set down passengers.

397. Red rear reflectors show up when headlights shine on them. These are useful when you're parked at night, but they'll only reflect if you park in the same direction as the traffic flow. Normally you should park on the left, but in a one-way street you may also park on the right-hand side.

398. You should normally use the left-hand lane on any dual carriageway unless you're overtaking or turning right.

399. There are times when road markings are obscured by queuing traffic, or you're unsure which lane to use. If, at the last moment, you find you're in the wrong lane, don't cut across or bully other drivers to let you in. Follow the lane you're in and find somewhere safe to turn around and rejoin your route.

400. You can overtake other traffic on either side when travelling in a one-way street. Make full use of your mirrors and ensure it's clear all around before you attempt to overtake. Look for signs and road markings, and use the most suitable lane for your destination.

401. When going straight ahead at a roundabout, don't signal as you approach it. Indicate left just after passing the exit before the one you wish to take.

402. A long vehicle may have to straddle lanes either on or approaching a roundabout so that the rear wheels don't hit the kerb.

403. Yellow box junctions are marked on the road to prevent the road becoming blocked. Don't enter the box unless your exit road is clear. You may wait in the box if you want to turn right and your exit road is clear but oncoming traffic or other vehicles waiting to turn right are preventing you from making the turn.

404. The purpose of yellow box markings is to keep junctions clear of queuing traffic. You may only wait in the marked area when you're turning right and your exit lane is clear but you can't complete the turn because of oncoming traffic or other traffic waiting to turning right.

405. You must obey signals to stop given by police and traffic officers, traffic wardens and school crossing patrols. Failure to do so is an offence and could lead to prosecution.

406. By standing on the pavement, the pedestrian is showing an intention to cross. By looking well ahead, you'll give yourself time to see the pedestrian, check your mirrors and respond safely.

407. Toucan crossings are similar to pelican crossings but there's no flashing amber phase. Cyclists share the crossing with pedestrians and are allowed to cycle across when the green cycle symbol is shown.

408. This light allows pedestrians already on the crossing to get to the other side in their own time, without being rushed. Don't rev your engine or start to move off while they're still crossing.

409. When turning right at a crossroads where oncoming traffic is also turning right, it's generally safer to turn behind the approaching vehicle. This allows you a clear view of approaching traffic and is called 'turning offside to offside'. However, some junctions, usually controlled by traffic-light filters - are marked for vehicles to turn nearside to nearside.

410. Travel slowly and carefully near parked vehicles. Beware of vehicles pulling out.

411. Take care if you have to pass a parked vehicle on your side of the road. Give way to oncoming traffic if there isn't enough room for you both to continue safely.

412. Normally you should travel in the left-hand lane and only use the right-hand lane for overtaking or turning right. Move back into the left lane as soon as it's safe but don't cut in across the path of the vehicle you've just passed.

413. Practise good observation in all directions before you emerge or make a turn. Proceed only when you're sure it's safe to do so.

414. Don't park within 10 metres (32 feet) of a junction (unless in an authorised parking place). This is to allow drivers emerging from, or turning into, the junction a clear view of the road they're joining. It also allows them to see hazards such as pedestrians or cyclists at the junction.

415. It may be tempting to park where you shouldn't while you run a quick errand. Careless parking is a selfish act and could endanger other road users. It's important not to park at or near a bus stop, as this could inconvenience passengers and may put them at risk as they get on or off the bus.

416. If the lights at a level crossing keep flashing after a train has passed, you should continue to wait, because another train might be coming. Time seems to pass slowly when you're held up in a queue. Be patient and wait until the lights stop flashing.

417. Where there are extra hazards, such as at roadworks, it's often necessary to slow traffic down by imposing a lower speed limit. These speed limits aren't advisory; they must be obeyed.

418. You may be difficult to see when you're travelling at night, even on a well-lit road. If you use dipped headlights rather than sidelights, other road users should be able to see you more easily.

419. When the central reservation is narrow, you should treat a dual carriageway as one road. Wait until the road is clear in both directions before emerging to turn right. If you try to treat it as two separate roads and wait in the middle, you're likely to cause an obstruction and possibly a collision.

420. Exceeding the speed limit is dangerous and can result in you receiving penalty points on your licence. It isn't worth it. You should know the speed limit for the road that you're on by observing the road signs. Different speed limits apply if you're towing a trailer.

421. You must use parking lights when parking at night on a road or in a lay-by on a road with a speed limit greater than 30 mph. You must also park in the direction of the traffic flow and not close to a junction.

422. You'll find traffic officers on England's motorways. They work in partnership with the police, helping to keep traffic moving and helping to make your journey as safe as possible. It's an offence not to comply with the directions given by a traffic officer.

423. To go straight ahead at a roundabout, you should normally approach in the left-hand lane, but check the road markings. At some roundabouts, the left lane on approach is marked 'left turn only', so make sure you use the correct lane to go ahead. You won't normally need to signal as you approach, but signal before you leave the roundabout, as other road users need to know your intentions.

424. It's illegal to drive on or over a footpath, except to gain access to a property. If you need to cross a pavement, give priority to pedestrians.

425. The speed limit for cars towing caravans or trailers on dual carriageways or motorways is 60 mph. Due to the increased weight and size of the combination, you should plan further ahead. Take care in windy weather, as a strong side wind can make a caravan or large trailer unstable.

426. Leave the lane free for cyclists. At other times, when the lane isn't in operation, you should still be aware that there may be cyclists about. Give them plenty of room as you pass and allow for their movement from side to side, especially in windy weather or on a bumpy road.

427. Your road position can help other road users to anticipate your actions. Keep to the left as you approach a left turn and don't swing out into the centre of the road in order to make the turn easier. This could endanger oncoming traffic and may cause other road users to misunderstand your intentions.

428. At a level crossing, flashing red lights mean you must stop. If the train passes but the lights keep flashing, wait. Another train may be coming.

429. Keep going; don't stop on the crossing. If the amber warning lights come on as you're approaching the crossing, you must stop unless it's unsafe to do so. Red flashing lights together with an audible signal mean you must stop.

430. Don't turn around in a busy street or reverse from a side road into a main road. Find a quiet side road and choose a place where you won't obstruct an entrance or exit. Look out for pedestrians and cyclists as well as other traffic.

431. You may remove your seat belt while you're carrying out a manoeuvre that includes reversing. However, you must remember to put it back on again before you resume driving.

432. You mustn't reverse further than is necessary. You may decide to turn your vehicle around by reversing into an opening or side road. When you reverse, always look all around you, and watch for pedestrians. Don't reverse from a side road into a main road.

433. A small child could be hidden directly behind you, so, if you can't see all around your vehicle, get out and have a look. You could also ask someone reliable outside the vehicle to guide you.

434. Don't reverse into a main road from a side road. The main road is likely to be busy and the traffic on it moving quickly.

435. You can wait in the box junction as long as your exit is clear. At some point there'll be a gap in the oncoming traffic, or the traffic lights will change, allowing you to proceed.

436. Always check in all directions before reversing into a side road. Keep a good lookout throughout the manoeuvre. Act on what you see and wait if necessary.

437. If you have a garage, use it. Your vehicle is less likely to be a victim of car crime if it's in a garage. Also, in winter, the windows will be kept free from ice and snow.

438. Urban clearways have their times of operation clearly signed. You may stop only for as long as is reasonable to pick up or set down passengers. You should ensure that you're not causing an obstruction for other traffic.

439. It's illegal to park in a space reserved for disabled users unless you're permitted to do so. These spaces are provided for people with limited mobility, who may need extra space to get in and out of their vehicle.

440. Pull into the nearest passing place on the left if you meet another vehicle on a narrow road. If the nearest passing place is on the right, wait opposite it.

441. On full beam, your lights could dazzle the driver in front. Dip your lights as soon as the driver passes you and drop back so that the dipped beam falls short of the other vehicle.

442. Your brake lights will give an indication to traffic behind that you're slowing down. Good anticipation will allow you time to check your mirrors before slowing.

443. Make sure you carry out the manoeuvre without causing a hazard to other vehicles. Choose a place to turn that's safe and convenient for you and for other road users.

444. Whenever possible, park in an area that will be well lit at night.

445. Keep a lookout for traffic signs. If you're directed to change lanes, do so in good time. Don't push your way into traffic and other lanes.

446. Cycle lanes are marked with either a solid or a broken white line. If the line is solid, you should check the times of operation shown on the signs, and not drive or park in the lane during those times. If the line is broken, you shouldn't drive or park in the lane unless it's unavoidable.

447. Don't park in a space reserved for disabled people unless you or your passenger are a disabled badge holder. The badge must be displayed in your vehicle, in the bottom left-hand corner of the windscreen.

448. You must stop your vehicle when signalled to do so by a police officer, traffic warden, school crossing patrol or red traffic light.

449. There are three basic types of traffic sign: those that warn, those that inform and those that give orders. Generally, triangular signs warn, rectangular signs give information or directions and circular signs give orders. An exception is the eight-sided 'stop' sign.

450. Some garages will remind you that your vehicle is due for its annual MOT test, but not all do. To ensure continuous cover, you may take your vehicle for its MOT up to one month before its existing MOT certificate runs out. The expiry date on the new certificate will be 12 months after the expiry date on the old certificate.

451. Sometimes an insurance company will issue a temporary insurance certificate called a cover note. It gives you the same insurance cover as your certificate but lasts for a limited period, usually one month.

452. If you accumulate six or more penalty points within two years of gaining your first full licence, it will be revoked. The six or more points include any gained due to offences you committed before passing your test. If this happens, you may only drive as a learner until you pass both the theory and practical tests again.

453. A SORN allows you to keep a vehicle off-road and untaxed. SORN will end when the vehicle is taxed, sold or scrapped.

454. If you want to keep a vehicle untaxed and off the public road, you must make a SORN. It's an offence not to do so. Your SORN is valid until your vehicle is taxed, sold or scrapped.

455. Driving without insurance is a serious offence. As well as an unlimited fine, you may be disqualified or incur penalty points.

456. It's your legal responsibility to keep the details on your vehicle registration certificate (V5C) up to date. You should tell the licensing authority about any changes. These include your name, address or vehicle details. If you don't do this, you may have problems when you try to sell your vehicle.

457. You must produce a valid insurance certificate when requested by a police officer. If you can't do this immediately, you may be asked to take it to a police station. Other documents you may be asked to produce are your driving licence and the vehicle's MOT certificate.

458. Using a vehicle on the road illegally carries a heavy fine and can lead to penalty points on your driving licence. You must have a valid driving license, paid the appropriate vehicle tax, and have proper insurance cover.

459. You can renew your vehicle tax online, at post offices and vehicle registration offices, or by phone. When applying, make sure you have all the relevant valid documents, including a valid MOT test certificate where applicable.

460. You don't have to carry around your vehicle's documents wherever you go. If a police officer asks to see them and you don't have them with you, you may be asked to produce them at a police station within 7 days.

461. Driving a vehicle without insurance cover is illegal, so be sure that, whoever's car you drive, you're insured – whether on their policy or on your own. If you need to take out insurance, it's worth comparing several quotes before you decide which insurance provider best meets your needs.

462. If your vehicle requires an MOT certificate, it's illegal to drive it without one and your insurance may be invalid if you do so. The only exceptions are that you may drive to a pre-arranged MOT test appointment, or to a garage for repairs required for the test.

463. It's your responsibility to make sure you're properly insured for the vehicle you're driving. This is the case regardless of whether you're a newly qualified driver or one with more experience.

464. Third-party insurance doesn't cover damage to your own vehicle or injury to yourself. If you have a crash and your vehicle is damaged, you might have to carry out the repairs at your own expense.

465. The registered keeper of the vehicle is responsible for paying the vehicle tax or making a Statutory Off-Road Notification (SORN) if the vehicle is to be kept untaxed and off the road.

466. Every vehicle used on the road has a registration document. This shows the vehicle's details, including date of first registration, registration number, registered keeper, previous keeper, make of vehicle, engine size, chassis number, year of manufacture and colour.

467. The licensing authority needs to keep its records up to date. It sends out a reminder when a vehicle's tax is due for renewal. To do this, it needs to know the name and address of the registered keeper. Every vehicle in the country is registered, so it's possible to trace its history.

468. The licensing authorities hold the records of all vehicles, drivers and riders in Great Britain and Northern Ireland. They need to know if you have a medical condition that might affect your ability to drive safely. You must tell them if your health deteriorates and you become unfit to drive.

469. The cost of insurance varies with your age and how long you've been driving. Usually, the younger you are, the more expensive it is, especially if you're under 25.

470. Learner drivers benefit by combining professional driving lessons with private practice. However, you need to be at least 21 years old and have held your driving licence for at least 3 years before you can supervise a learner driver.

471. When a car is three years old (four years old in Northern Ireland), it must pass an MOT test and have a valid MOT certificate before it can be used on the road, unless you are driving to a pre-arranged appointment.

472. The vehicle you drive must be roadworthy and in good condition. If it's over three years old, it must pass an MOT test to remain in use on the road (unless it's exempt from the MOT test - see GOV.UK).

473. New drivers are far more vulnerable on the road and more likely to be involved in incidents. The Pass Plus scheme has been designed to improve new drivers' basic skills and help widen their driving experience.

474. Third-party insurance cover is usually cheaper than comprehensive cover. However, it doesn't cover any damage caused to your own vehicle or property. It only covers damage and injury you cause to others.

475. The minimum insurance required by law is third-party cover. This covers your liability to others involved in a collision but not damage to your vehicle. Basic third-party insurance also won't cover theft or fire damage. Ask your insurance company for advice on the best cover for you and make sure that you read the policy carefully.

476. Having an excess on your policy will help to keep the premium down. However, if you make a claim, you'll have to pay the excess yourself – in this case, £100.

477. After passing your practical driving test, you can take further training. One option is known as the Pass Plus scheme. It's designed to improve your basic driving skills and involves a series of modules, including night-time and motorway driving.

478. The Pass Plus scheme was created for newly qualified drivers. It aims to widen their driving experience and improve basic skills. After passing the practical driving test, additional professional training can be taken with an approved driving instructor (ADI). Some insurance companies also offer discounts to holders of a Pass Plus certificate.

479. If a disabled driver's vehicle breaks down and they're unable to walk to an emergency phone, they're advised to stay in their car and switch on the hazard warning lights. They may also display a 'help' pennant in their vehicle.

480. Hazard warning lights are fitted to all modern cars and some motorcycles. They should be used to warn other drivers of a hazard, or if you have broken down.

481. You mustn't use hazard warning lights while moving, except to warn traffic behind when you slow suddenly on a motorway or unrestricted dual carriageway.

482. It's important to keep a safe distance from the vehicle in front at all times. This still applies in congested tunnels, even if you're moving very slowly or have stopped. If the vehicle in front breaks down, you may need room to manoeuvre past it.

483. The hard shoulder should only be used in a genuine emergency. If possible, and if it's safe, use a roadside telephone to call for help. This will give your exact location to the operator. Never cross the carriageway or a slip road to use a telephone on the other side of the road.

484. If possible, lay the casualty down. Protect yourself from exposure to blood and, when you're sure there's nothing in the wound, apply firm pressure to it using clean material.

485. If a casualty is unconscious, you need to check that they're breathing normally. Look for chest movements, look and listen for breathing, and feel for breath on your cheek.

486. Check the casualty for shock and, if possible, try to cool the burn for at least 10 minutes using clean, cool water.

487. If a casualty isn't breathing normally, cardiopulmonary resuscitation (CPR) may be needed to maintain circulation. Place two hands on the centre of the chest and press down hard and fast – around 5–6 centimetres and about twice a second.

488. The effects of shock may not be immediately obvious. Warning signs are rapid pulse, sweating, pale grey skin and rapid shallow breathing.

489. After a casualty has been placed in the recovery position, make sure their airway remains open and monitor their condition until medical help arrives. Where possible, don't move a casualty unless there's further danger.

490. If someone has been injured, the sooner proper medical attention is given the better. Ask someone to phone for help or do it yourself. An injured person should only be moved if they're in further danger. An injured motorcyclist's helmet shouldn't be removed unless it's essential.

491. Lorry drivers can be unaware of objects falling from their vehicles. If you see something fall onto a motorway, look to see if the driver pulls over. If they don't stop, don't attempt to retrieve the object yourself. Pull onto the hard shoulder near an emergency telephone and report the hazard.

492. Follow the instructions given by the signs or by tunnel officials. In congested tunnels, a minor incident can soon turn into a major one, with serious or even fatal results.

493. An adult casualty isn't breathing normally. To maintain circulation, place two hands on the centre of the chest. Then press down hard and fast – around 5–6 centimetres and about twice a second.

494. At a crash scene you can help in practical ways, even if you aren't trained in first aid. Call the emergency services and make sure you don't put yourself or anyone else in danger. The safest way to warn other traffic is by switching on your hazard warning lights.

495. If you're the first to arrive at a crash scene, the first concerns are the risk of further collision and fire. Ensuring that vehicle engines are switched off will reduce the risk of fire. Use hazard warning lights so that other traffic knows there's a need for caution. Make sure the emergency services are contacted; don't assume this has already been done.

496. Don't remove a motorcyclist's helmet unless it's essential. Remember they may be suffering from shock. Don't give them anything to eat or drink, but do reassure them confidently.

497. At the scene of an incident, always be aware of danger from further collisions or fire. The first priority when dealing with an unconscious person is to ensure they're breathing normally. If they're having difficulty breathing, follow the DR ABC code.

498. Remember this procedure by saying DR ABC. This stands for Danger, Response, Airway, Breathing, Circulation. Give whatever first aid you can and stay with the injured person until the emergency services arrive.

499. There are a number of things you can do to help, even without expert training. Be aware of further danger from other traffic and fire; make sure the area is safe. People may be in shock. Don't give them anything to eat or drink. Keep them warm and comfortable and reassure them. Don't move injured people unless there's a risk of further danger.

500. A casualty suffering from shock may have injuries that aren't immediately obvious. Call the emergency services, then stay with the person in shock, offering reassurance until the experts arrive.

501. The motorcyclist is in an extremely vulnerable position, exposed to further danger from traffic. Approaching vehicles need advance warning in order to slow down and safely take avoiding action or stop. Don't put yourself or anyone else at risk. Use the hazard warning lights on your vehicle to alert other road users to the danger.

502. If a young child has stopped breathing, first check that their airway is open and then begin CPR. With a young child, you may only need to use one hand and you shouldn't press down as far as you would with an adult. Continue the procedure until the child is breathing again or until a medical professional takes over.

503. It's important to ensure that the airway is open before you start CPR. To open the casualty's airway, place your fingers under their chin and lift it forward.

504. Your priority is to cool the burns with clean, cool water. Its coolness will help take the heat out of the burns and relieve the pain. Keep the wound doused for at least 10 minutes. If blisters appear, don't attempt to burst them, as this could lead to infection.

505. If there's nothing in the wound, applying firm pressure using a pad of clean cloth or bandage will help stem the bleeding. Don't tie anything tightly round the leg, as this will restrict circulation and could result in long-term injury.

506. Don't move a casualty unless there's further danger; for example, from other traffic or fire. They may have unseen or internal injuries. Moving them unnecessarily could cause further injury. Don't remove a motorcyclist's helmet unless it's essential.

507. When the area is safe and there's no danger from other traffic or fire, it's better not to move casualties. Moving them may cause further injury.

508. You must stop if you've been involved in a collision which results in injury or damage. The police may ask to see your driving licence and insurance details at the time or later at a police station.

509. It's important to make sure that the emergency services arrive as soon as possible. When a person is unconscious, they could have serious injuries that aren't immediately obvious.

510. The most immediate danger is further collisions and fire. You could warn other traffic by switching on hazard warning lights, displaying an advance warning triangle or sign (but not on a motorway), or by any other means that doesn't put you or others at risk.

511. The DR ABC code has been devised by medical experts to give the best outcome until the emergency services arrive and take care of casualties.

512. If someone is suffering from shock, try to keep them warm and as comfortable as you can. Don't give them anything to eat or drink but reassure them confidently and try not to leave them alone.

513. When someone is injured, any movement that isn't absolutely necessary should be avoided, since it could make the injuries worse. Unless it's essential to remove a motorcyclist's helmet, it's generally safer to leave it in place.

514. Advance warning triangles fold flat and don't take up much room. Use one to warn other road users if your vehicle has broken down or if there has been an incident. Place it at least 45 metres (147 feet) behind your vehicle (or the incident), on the same side of the road or verge. Place it further back if the scene is hidden by, for example, a bend, hill or dip in the road. Don't use warning triangles on motorways.

515. If your vehicle breaks down on a level crossing, your first priority is to get everyone out of the vehicle and clear of the crossing. Then use the railway telephone, if there is one, to tell the signal operator. If you have time before the train arrives, move the vehicle clear of the crossing, but only do this if alarm signals are not on.

516. A tyre bursting can lead to a loss of control, especially if you're travelling at high speed. Using the correct procedure should help you to stop the vehicle safely.

517. Pull up on the hard shoulder and make your way to the nearest emergency telephone to call for assistance.

518. Try to stay calm, especially if you have passengers with you. If you can't restart your engine before the warning bells ring, leave the vehicle and get yourself and any passengers well clear of the crossing.

519. Briefly using your hazard warning lights will warn the traffic travelling behind you that there's a hazard ahead. This can reduce the chance of vehicles crashing into the back of each other.

520. Have the correct details ready before you use the emergency telephone. The operator will need to know the details of your vehicle and its fault. For your own safety, always face the traffic when you speak on a roadside telephone.

521. If you're wearing sunglasses, you should remove them before driving into a tunnel. If you don't, your vision will be restricted, even in tunnels that appear to be well lit.

522. Before entering a tunnel, you should switch on your dipped headlights, as this will allow you to see and be seen. In many tunnels, it's a legal requirement.

523. The fuel in your vehicle can be a dangerous fire hazard. If you smell fuel, check out where it's coming from. Never use a naked flame or smoke if you smell fuel.

524. If any object falls onto the motorway carriageway from your vehicle, pull onto the hard shoulder near an emergency telephone and call for assistance. Don't stop on the carriageway or attempt to retrieve anything.

525. Make sure you know what the different warning lights mean. An illuminated warning light could mean that your car is unsafe to drive. If you aren't sure about the problem, get a qualified mechanic to check it.

526. If your vehicle breaks down, get help without delay. Switch on your hazard warning lights, then go to an emergency telephone to call for help.

527. If it's possible, and you can do so without causing further danger, it may be safer to drive a vehicle that's on fire out of a tunnel. The greatest danger in a tunnel fire is smoke and suffocation.

528. It's usually better to drive a burning vehicle out of a tunnel. If you can't do this, pull over and stop at an emergency point if possible. Switch off the engine, use hazard warning lights, and leave the vehicle immediately. Call for help from the nearest emergency point. If you have an extinguisher it may help to put out a small fire, but don't try to tackle a large one.

529. On the approach to tunnels, a sign will usually show a local radio channel. This should give a warning of any incidents or congestion in the tunnel ahead. Many radios can be set to automatically pick up traffic announcements and local frequencies. If you have to tune the radio manually, don't be distracted while doing so. Incidents in tunnels can lead to serious casualties. The greatest hazard is fire. Getting an advance warning of problems could save your life and others.

530. First, get yourself and anyone else well away from the crossing. If there's a railway telephone, use that to get instructions from the signal operator. Then, if there's time, move the vehicle clear of the crossing.

531. Various items – such as a first aid kit and a fire extinguisher – can provide invaluable help in the event of a collision or breakdown. They could even save a life.

532. If you're in a collision that causes damage or injury to any other person, vehicle, animal or property, by law you must stop. Give your name, the vehicle owner's name and address, and the vehicle's registration number to anyone who has reasonable grounds for requesting them.

533. Try to keep calm and don't rush. Make sure that you've shared all the relevant details with the other driver before you leave the scene. If possible, take pictures and note the positions of all the vehicles involved.

534. If the property owner isn't available at the time, you must inform the police about the incident. This should be done as soon as possible, and in any case within 24 hours.

535. The motorway regulations for towing a trailer state that you mustn't use the right hand lane of a three lane motorway or exceed 60 mph

536. Strong winds or buffeting from large vehicles can cause a trailer or caravan to swing from side to side ('snake'). If this happens, ease off the accelerator. Don't brake harshly, steer sharply or increase your speed.

537. Check the vehicle handbook. This should give you guidance on the correct tyre pressures for your vehicle and when you may need to adjust them. If you're carrying a heavy load, you may need to adjust the headlights as well. Most cars have a switch on the dashboard to do this.

538. A heavy load on your roof rack will reduce the stability of the vehicle because it moves the centre of gravity away from that designed by the manufacturer. Be aware of this when you drive round bends and corners. If you change direction at speed, your vehicle and/or load could become unstable and you could lose control.

539. Any load will have an effect on the handling of your vehicle, and this becomes worse as you increase the load. You need to be aware of this when carrying passengers or heavy loads, fitting a roof rack or towing a trailer.

540. Carrying heavy loads will affect control and the vehicle's handling characteristics. If the vehicle you're driving is overloaded, you'll be held responsible.

541. Towing a caravan or trailer affects the way the towing vehicle handles. A stabiliser device is not designed to overcome instability caused by incorrect loading but it can give added security in side winds and from buffeting caused by large vehicles.

542. Riding in a towed caravan is highly dangerous. The safety of the entire unit is dependent on the stability of the trailer. Moving passengers would make the caravan unstable and could cause loss of control.

543. In the event that the trailer becomes detached from the towing vehicle, the breakaway cable activates the trailer brakes before snapping. This allows the towing vehicle to get free of the trailer and out of danger.

544. You must know how to load your trailer or caravan so that the hitch exerts an appropriate downward force on the tow ball. Information about the maximum permitted noseweight can be found in your vehicle handbook or obtained from your vehicle manufacturer's agent.

545. Any load must be securely fastened to the vehicle. The safest way to carry items on the roof is in a specially designed roof box.

546. It's your responsibility to ensure that all children in your car are secure. Suitable restraints include a child seat, baby seat, booster seat or booster cushion. It's essential that any restraint used is suitable for the child's size and weight, and fitted according to the manufacturer's instructions.

11453115R00109

Printed in Great Britain
by Amazon